HTML & CSS Essentials

by Paul McFedries

A Wiley Brand

HTML & CSS Essentials For Dummies®

Published by: **John Wiley & Sons, Inc.**, 111 River Street, Hoboken, NJ 07030-5774, www.wiley.com

Copyright © 2024 by John Wiley & Sons, Inc., Hoboken, New Jersey

Published simultaneously in Canada

For general information on our other products and services, please contact our Customer Care Department within the U.S. at 877-762-2974, outside the U.S. at 317-572-3993, or fax 317-572-4002. For technical support, please visit https://hub.wiley.com/community/support/dummies.

Wiley publishes in a variety of print and electronic formats and by print-on-demand. Some material included with standard print versions of this book may not be included in e-books or in print-on-demand. If this book refers to media such as a CD or DVD that is not included in the version you purchased, you may download this material at http://booksupport.wiley.com. For more information about Wiley products, visit www.wiley.com.

Library of Congress Control Number: 2024934074

ISBN 978-1-394-26290-8 (pbk); ISBN 978-1-394-26292-2 (ebk); ISBN 978-1-394-26291-5 (ebk)

SKY10072502_041224

Contents at a Glance

Table of Contents

Introduction

Let me start off this book by letting you in on a little secret. If you talk to or read things written by people who make websites for a living, it's all "HTML this" and "CSS that." They go on and on about "tags" and "properties" and "collapsing margins" and blah blah blah. It can be more than a little intimidating, so you can easily come away with the idea that crafting a web page is *really* hard. You may end up believing that creating stuff for the web is a for-geeks-with-CS-graduate-degrees-only business.

Okay, it's time for that secret I just promised you. Ready? Come closer. Closer. Okay:

whispers *Learning how to build web pages is not hard.*

Sure, it *sounds* hard; and if you've ever taken a peek at some web page code, it certainly *looks* hard; and, I'll admit, building a huge and insanely complex site like Amazon or Instagram really *is* hard. But creating a personal website? Not hard. Fabricating a site to showcase a hobby? Not hard. Crafting some pages for a local charity, team, or small business? You got it: Not hard!

Still don't believe me? That's okay, I get it: HTML and CSS — the technologies that enable anyone to assemble web pages — have a reputation problem. After all, so the thinking goes, people have used HTML and CSS to sculpt some truly sensational sites, so *of course* such sophistication must come with a near-vertical learning curve. Duh.

For years now I've talked to many smart people who believed all that and who therefore wouldn't even dream of building a web page from scratch. How many awesome websites never got built because their would-be builders thought HTML and CSS were well beyond their capabilities? Why is no one talking about how accessible these technologies really are?

After asking myself these questions over and over, I finally decided to do something about it. I decided to write this book, the aim of which is to prove to everyone — yes, even skeptical you — that the technologies behind the web are approachable, straightforward, and readily learnable.

About This Book

Welcome, then, to *HTML & CSS Essentials For Dummies*. This book gives you a solid education on the technologies that enable anyone to craft professional-looking web pages. You learn how to set up the tools you need and how to use HTML and CSS to design and build your site. My goal is to show you that these technologies aren't hard to learn, and that even the greenest rookie web designer can learn how to put together pages that will amaze their family and friends (and themselves).

If you're looking for lots of programming history, computer science theory, and long-winded explanations of concepts, I'm sorry, but you won't find it here. My philosophy throughout this book comes from Linus Torvalds, the creator of the Linux operating system: "Talk is cheap. Show me the code." I explain what needs to be explained and then I move on without further ado (or, most of the time, without any ado at all) to examples that do more to illuminate a concept that any verbose explanations I could muster (and believe me, I can muster verbosity with the best of them).

Foolish Assumptions

This book is not a primer on the internet or on using the World Wide Web. This is a book on building web pages, pure and simple. This means I assume the following:

>> You know how to operate a basic text editor, and how to get around the operating system and file system on your computer.

>> You have an internet connection.

>> You know how to use your web browser.

Yep, that's it.

Icons Used in This Book

This icon points out juicy tidbits that are likely to be repeatedly useful to you — so please don't forget them.

Think of these icons as the fodder of advice columns. They offer (hopefully) wise advice or a bit more information about a topic under discussion.

Look out! In this book, you see this icon when I'm trying to help you avoid mistakes that can cost you time, money, or embarrassment.

Where to Go from Here

How you approach this book depends on your current level of web coding expertise (or lack thereof):

>> If you're just starting out, begin at the beginning with Chapters 1 and 2. This will give you all the knowledge you need to pick and choose what you want to learn throughout the rest of the book.

>> If you know a bit of HTML and CSS, you can probably get away with taking a fast look at the first three chapters and then settle in with Chapter 4 and beyond.

Chapter **1**

Getting to Know HTML and CSS

This book is a sort of manual for using HTML and CSS. However, and this is particularly true if you're just getting started with coding web pages, if there's any part of the book that fits the old RTFM (read the freakin' manual) credo, it's this chapter. *Everything* you learn in this chapter acts as a kind of home base for the explorations that come later.

In this chapter, you learn the basic concepts behind HTML and CSS, get a better understanding of how they work, and get started exploring these powerful technologies.

Getting a Bird's-Eye View of the Process

You can add special codes inside a text file to specify how you want your web page to look. For example, maybe you want a particular collection of words or phrases to appear as a bulleted list. When the web browser comes to that part of the file, it dutifully renders those items as a list, bullets and all. The person browsing your page doesn't get the "render these items as a bulleted list" code; they just get the bulleted list. The web browser performs these and many other transformations behind the scenes. As long as you have the right HTML and CSS markings in the right places, the browser will render your page the way you want.

Launching a new text file

Your first step whenever you want to create a web page is to start a new text file. To do that, not surprisingly, you need to fire up your favorite text editor:

>> **Notepad (Windows):** In Windows 11, choose Start ⇨ All Apps ⇨ Notepad. Notepad displays a brand-new text file automatically when you start the program. You can also fire up a new document by choosing File ⇨ New.

>> **TextEdit (Mac):** Click Search (the magnifying glass) in the menu bar, start typing **textedit**, and then click TextEdit as soon as it shows up in the search results. In the dialog box that appears, click New Document. You can launch a new text file any time you need one by choosing File ⇨ New.

>> **Something else:** If you have another text editor, launch it the way you normally do and create a new file.

Saving HTML files

When it's time to save your work, here are a few notes to consider:

>> **Use the right file extension.** For garden-variety web pages, your file names must end with either the .htm or the .html file extension (for example, mypage.html).

>> **Use lowercase filenames without spaces.** For best results, always enter your filenames using only lowercase letters and don't use spaces in your filenames. If you want to separate words in file and directory names, use an underscore (_) or a hyphen (–).

>> **Use the right file type.** While in the Save As dialog box, you need to select the correct file type for your HTML file. How you do this depends on what program you're using. In most programs (including TextEdit), you use the File Format (or Save As Type) list to select Web Page (.html) or something similar. If you're using Notepad, use the Save As Type list to select All Files (*.*). This ensures that Notepad uses your .htm or .html extension (and not its normal .txt extension).

Edit. Save. Reload. Repeat.

Assuming that you've previously saved your HTML file as I describe in the previous section, your first task is to open the HTML file in your text editor and in your web browser:

» **Text editor:** Run the Open command (almost always by choosing File ➪ Open or by pressing Ctrl+O or ⌘+O) to open the HTML file you want to work with (if it's not open already, that is).

» **Web browser:** Run the Open command to load the same HTML file that you have open in your text editor. Finding the Open command is either trivial or tricky, depending on your operating system:

   • **Windows:** Whether you're using Edge, Chrome, or Firefox, press Ctrl+O to display the Open dialog box; then select the HTML file and click Open.

   • **macOS:** Whether you're using Safari, Chrome, or Firefox, choose File ➪ Open File (or press ⌘+O) to display the Open dialog; then select the HTML file and click Open.

With your HTML file open in both your text editor and your web browser, here's the basic cycle you use to build your pages:

1. **Add some text and HTML stuff (I define what this "stuff" is in the rest of this chapter) to your file.**

2. **Run the editor's Save command (almost always by choosing File ➪ Save or by pressing Ctrl+S or ⌘+S) to save your work.**

3. **Run the web browser's Reload command. Again, how you invoke Reload depends on the operating system:**

   • **Windows:** Whether you're using Edge, Chrome, or Firefox, press Ctrl+R to reload the page.

   • **macOS:** If you're using Safari or Chrome, choose View ➪ Reload Page (or press ⌘+R) to reload the page. In Firefox, press ⌘+R.

   The web browser reloads the page and displays whatever changes you made to the HTML file in Step 1.

4. **Repeat Steps 1 through 3 as often as you like.**

Getting to Know HTML

Building a web page from scratch using your bare hands may seem like a daunting task. It doesn't help that the codes you use to set up, configure, and format a web page are called the HyperText Markup Language (HTML for short), a name that could only warm the cockles of a geek's heart. Here's a mercifully brief look at each term:

>> **HyperText:** An oblique reference to the links that are the defining characteristic of web pages

>> **Markup:** The instructions that specify how the content of a web page should be displayed in the web browser

>> **Language:** The set of codes that comprise all the markup possibilities for a page

But even though the name HTML is intimidating, the codes used by HTML aren't even close to being hard to learn. There are only a few of them, and in many cases they even make sense!

Working with HTML elements and tags

At its most basic, HTML is nothing more than a collection of markup codes — called *elements* — that specify the structure of your web page. For most of your HTML chores, you create a kind of container. What types of things can reside in this container? Mostly text, although often they will be entire chunks of the web page and even other elements.

Most HTML containers use the following generic format:

```
<element>content</element>
```

What you have here are a couple of codes that define the container for a particular HTML element. Many elements are one- or two-letter abbreviations, but sometimes they're entire words. You always surround these elements with angle brackets <>; the brackets tell the web browser that it's dealing with a chunk of HTML and not just some random text. An element surrounded by angle brackets is called a *tag*.

An HTML code by itself is called an *element*; the element surrounded by angle brackets is known as a *tag*.

The first of these codes — `<element>` — is called the *start tag* and it marks the opening of the container; the second of the codes — `</element>` — is called the *end tag* and it marks the closing of the container. (Note the extra slash (/) that appears in the end tag.)

In between the start and end tags, you have the *content*, which refers to whatever is contained in the tag. For example, suppose you want to include in your page the sentence *This is a web page with something important to say*, and you want to punch this up a bit by emphasizing *important*. In HTML, the element for emphasis is em, so you'd type your sentence like so:

```
This is a web page with something <em>important
    </em> to say.
```

Notice how I've surrounded the word important with `<em>` and `</em>`? All web browsers display emphasized text in italics, so that's how the word appears, as shown in Figure 1-1.

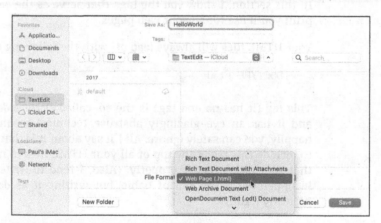

FIGURE 1-1: The sentence revised to italicize the word *important*.

There are tags for lots of other structures, including important text, paragraphs, headings, page titles, links, and lists. HTML is just the sum total of all these tags.

Dealing with tag attributes

You modify how a tag works by adding one or more *attributes* to the start tag. Most attributes use the following generic syntax:

```
<tag attribute="value">
```

Here, you replace `attribute` with the name of the attribute you want to apply to the tag, and you replace `value` with the value you want to assign the attribute, surrounded by either double or single quotation marks. If you add two or more attributes to a tag, be sure to separate each with a space.

For example, you use the `<a>` tag to create a link to another page and within the `<a>` tag you use the `href` attribute to specify the page address. Here's an example:

```
Go to <a href="rutabagas.html">my rutabagas page</a>
```

A barebones HTML page

In this section, I show you the tags that serve as the basic blueprint you'll use for all your web pages.

Your HTML files will always lead off with the following tag:

```
<!DOCTYPE html>
```

This tag (it has no end tag) is the so-called *Doctype declaration*, and it has an eye-glazingly abstruse technical meaning that, happily, you can safely ignore. All I'll say about it is that you have to include this tag at the top of all your HTML files to make sure that your pages render properly. (Also, I tend to write DOCTYPE in uppercase letters out of habit, but writing it as doctype is perfectly legal.)

Next up, you add the `<html lang="en">` tag. This tag doesn't do a whole lot except tell any web browser that tries to read the file that it's dealing with a file that contains HTML doodads. It also uses the `lang` attribute to specify the document's language, which in this case is English.

Similarly, the last line in your document will always be the corresponding end tag: `</html>`. You can think of this tag as the HTML equivalent for "The End." So, each of your web pages will include this on the second line:

```
<html lang="en">
```

and this on the last line:

```
</html>
```

The next items serve to divide the page into two sections: the head and the body. The head section is like an introduction to the page. Web browsers use the head to glean various types of information about the page. A number of items can appear in the head section, but the only one that makes any real sense at this early stage is the title of the page, which I talk about in the next section, "Giving your page a title."

To define the head, add <head> and </head> tags immediately below the <html> tag you typed in earlier. So, your web page should now look like this:

```
<!DOCTYPE html>
<html lang="en">
    <head>
    </head>
</html>
```

REMEMBER

Although technically it makes no difference if you enter your tag names in uppercase or lowercase letters, the HTML powers-that-be recommend HTML tags in lowercase letters, so that's the style I use in this book, and I encourage you to do the same.

REMEMBER

Notice that I indented the <head> and </head> tags a bit (by four spaces, actually). This indentation is good practice whenever you have HTML tags that reside within another HTML container because it makes your code easier to read and easier to troubleshoot.

While you're in the head section, here's an added head-scratcher:

```
<meta charset="utf-8">
```

You place this element between the <head> and </head> tags (indented another four spaces for easier reading). It tells the web browser that your web page uses the UTF-8 character set, which you can mostly ignore except to know that UTF-8 contains almost every character (domestic and foreign), punctuation mark, and symbol known to humankind.

The body section is where you enter the text and other fun stuff that the browser will actually display. To define the body, place <body> and </body> tags after the head section (that is, below the </head> tag):

```
<!DOCTYPE html>
<html lang="en">
    <head>
        <meta charset="utf-8">
    </head>
    <body>
    </body>
</html>
```

WARNING

A common page error is to include two or more copies of these basic tags, particularly the <body> tag. For best results, be sure you use each of these five basic structural tags — <!DOCTYPE>, <html>, <head>, <meta>, and <body> — only one time on each page.

Giving your page a title

When you surf the web, you've probably noticed that your browser displays some text in the current tab. That tab text is the web page title, which is a short (or sometimes long) phrase that gives the page a name. You can give your own web page a name by adding the <title> tag to the page's head section.

To define a title, surround the title text with the <title> and </title> tags. For example, if you want the title of your page to be "My Home Sweet Home Page," enter it as follows:

```
<title>My Home Sweet Home Page</title>
```

Note that you always place the title inside the head section, so your basic HTML document now looks like this:

```
<!DOCTYPE html>
<html lang="en">
    <head>
        <meta charset="utf-8">
        <title>My Home Sweet Home Page</title>
    </head>
    <body>
    </body>
</html>
```

Figure 1-2 shows this HTML file loaded into a web browser. Notice how the title appears in the browser's tab bar.

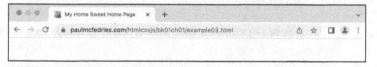

FIGURE 1-2: The text you insert into the `<title>` tag shows up in the browser tab.

Here are a few things to keep in mind when thinking of a title for your page:

>> Be sure your title describes what the page is all about.

>> Don't make your title too long. If you do, the browser may chop it off because the tab doesn't have enough room to display it. Fifty or 60 characters are usually the max.

>> Use titles that make sense when someone views them out of context. For example, if someone really likes your page, that person may add it to their list of favorites or bookmarks. The browser displays the page title in the Favorites list, so it's important that the title makes sense when a viewer looks at the bookmarks later on.

>> Don't use cryptic or vague titles. Titling a page "Link #42" or "My Web Page" may make sense to you, but your visitors will almost certainly be scratching their heads.

Adding some text

Now it's time to put some flesh on your web page's bones by entering the text you want to appear in the body of the page. For the most part, you can type the text between the ⟨body⟩ and ⟨/body⟩ tags, like this (refer to bk01ch01/example04.html):

```
<!DOCTYPE html>
<html lang="en">
    <head>
        <meta charset="utf-8">
        <title>My Home Sweet Home Page</title>
    </head>
    <body>
        Hello HTML World!
    </body>
</html>
```

Figure 1-3 shows how a web browser displays this HTML.

FIGURE 1-3: Text you add to the page body appears in the browser's content window.

Before you start typing, however, there are a few things you should know:

>> You may think you can line things up and create some interesting effects by stringing together two or more spaces. Ha! Web browsers chew up all those extra spaces and spit them out into the nether regions of cyberspace. Why? Well, the philosophy of the web is that you can use only HTML elements to lay out a document. So, a run of multiple spaces (or *white space,* as it's called) is ignored.

>> Tabs also fall under the rubric of white space. You can enter tabs all day long, but the browser ignores them completely.

>> Browsers also like to ignore the carriage return. It may sound reasonable to the likes of you and me that pressing Enter (or

Return on a Mac) starts a new paragraph, but that's not so in the HTML world.

>> If you want to separate two chunks of text, you have multiple ways to go, but here are the two easiest:

- **For no space between the texts:** Place a ‹br› (for line break) tag between the two bits of text.

- **For some breathing room between the texts:** Surround each chunk of text with the ‹p› and ‹/p› (for paragraph) tags.

>> If HTML documents are just plain text, does that mean you're out of luck if you need to use characters such as © and €? Luckily, no. For the most part, you can just add these characters to your file. However, HTML also has special codes for these kinds of characters.

>> If, for some reason, you're using a word processor instead of a text editor, know that it won't help to format your text using the program's built-in commands. The browser cheerfully ignores even the most elaborate formatting jobs because browsers understand only HTML (and CSS and JavaScript). And besides, a document with formatting is, by definition, not a pure text file, so a browser may have trouble loading it.

Getting Familiar with CSS

One of the things that makes web coding with HTML so addictive is that you can slap up a page using a few basic tags and find that it usually works pretty good when you examine the result in the browser. A work of art it's not, but it won't make your eyes sore. The browsers' default formatting means that even a basic page looks reasonable, but I'm betting you're reading this book because you want to shoot for something more than reasonable. In this section, you discover that the secret to creating great-looking pages is to override the default browser formatting with your own. You do that by augmenting your pages with some CSS.

Understanding cascading style sheets

If you want to control the look of your web pages, the royal road to that goal is a web-coding technology called *cascading style sheets*, or *CSS*. Before getting to the specifics, I answer three simple questions: What's a style? What's a sheet? What's a cascade?

Styles: Bundles of formatting options

In a nutshell, a *style* is a bundle of formatting options rolled into one nice, neat package. That is, it enables you to define a series of formatting options for a given page element, such as a tag like `<div>` or `<h1>`.

Sheets: Collections of styles

The term *style sheet* harkens back to the days of yore when old-timey publishing firms would keep track of their preferences for things like typefaces, type sizes, margins, and so on. All these so-called "house styles" were stored in a manual known as a *style sheet*. On the web, a style sheet is similar: It's a collection styles that you can apply to a web page.

Cascading: How styles propagate

The "cascading" part of the name *cascading style sheets* is a bit technical, but it refers to a mechanism that's built into CSS for propagating styles between elements.

Getting comfy with CSS rules and declarations

Before I show you how to actually use CSS in your web pages, take a second to get a grip on just what a style looks like.

The simplest case is to apply a single formatting option to an element. Here's the general syntax for this:

```
element {
    property: value;
}
```

Here, `element` is a reference to the web page doodad to which you want the style applied. This reference is often a tag name (such as h1 or div), but CSS has a powerful toolbox of ways you can reference things, which I discuss in Chapter 6.

The *property* part is the name of the CSS property you want to apply. CSS offers a large collection of properties, each of which is a short, alphabetic keyword, such as font-family for the typeface, color for the text color, and border-width for the thickness of a border. The property name is followed by a colon (:), a space for readability, the *value* you want to assign to the property, and then a semicolon (;). This line of code is known in the trade as a *CSS declaration.*

REMEMBER

Always enter the *property* name using lowercase letters. If the *value* includes any characters other than letters or a hyphen, you need to surround the value with quotation marks (single or double).

Notice, too, that the declaration is surrounded by braces ({ and }). You can place multiple declarations between the braces, and that collection is known as a *declaration block.* A declaration block applied to a page item (such as an HTML element) is called a *style rule.*

For example, the following rule applies a 72-pixel (indicated by the px unit) font size to the <h1> tag:

```
h1 {
    font-size: 72px;
}
```

The following example shows a rule with multiple declarations:

```
h1 {
    border-width: 1px;
    border-style: solid;
    border-color: black;
    font-family: Verdana;
    font-size: 72px;
    text-align: center;
}
```

Besides applying multiple styles to a single item, it's also possible to apply a single style to multiple items. You set up the style in the usual way, but instead of a single item at the beginning of the rule, you list all the items that you want to style, separated by commas:

```
header,
aside,
footer {
    background-color: yellow;
}
```

Applying styles to a page

With HTML tags, you just plop the tag where you want it to appear on the page, but styles aren't quite so straightforward. In fact, there are three main ways to get your web page styled: inline styles, internal style sheets, and external style sheets.

Inserting inline styles

An *inline style* is a style rule that you insert directly into whatever tag you want to format. Here's the general syntax to use:

```
<element style="property1: value1; property2:
    value2; ...">
```

That is, you add the `style` attribute to your tag, and then set it equal to one or more declarations, separated by semicolons.

For example, to apply 72-pixel type to an `<h1>` heading, you could add an inline style that uses the `font-size` CSS property:

```
<h1 style="font-size: 72px;">
```

Embedding an internal style sheet

For easier maintenance of your styles, and to take advantage of the many ways that CSS offers to apply a single style rule to multiple page items, you need to turn to style sheets, which can be either internal (as I discuss here) or external (as I discuss in the next section).

An *internal style sheet* is a style sheet that resides within the same file as the page's HTML code. Specifically, the style sheet is embedded between the `<style>` and `</style>` tags in the page's head section, like so:

```
<!DOCTYPE html>
<html lang="en">
    <head>
        <style>
            Your style rules go here
        </style>
    </head>
    <body>
    ...
```

Here's the general syntax to use:

```
<style>
    itemA {
        propertyA1: valueA1;
        propertyA2: valueA2;
        ...
    }
    itemB {
        propertyB1: valueB1;
        propertyB2: valueB2;
        ...
    }
    ...
</style>
```

As the preceding code shows, an internal style sheet consists of one or more style rules embedded within a `<style>` tag, which is why an internal style sheet is also sometimes called an *embedded style sheet*.

In the following code, I apply border styles to the h1 and h2 elements: solid and dotted, respectively. Figure 1-4 shows the result.

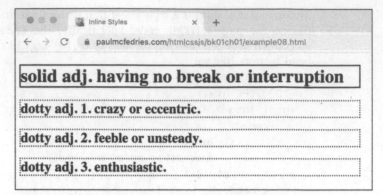

FIGURE 1-4: An internal style sheet that applies different border styles to the h1 (top) and h2 elements.

HTML:

```
<h1>solid adj. having no break or interruption</h1>
<h2>dotty adj. 1. crazy or eccentric.</h2>
<h2>dotty adj. 2. feeble or unsteady.</h2>
<h2>dotty adj. 3. enthusiastic.</h2>
```

CSS:

```
<style>
    h1 {
        border-width: 2px;
        border-style: solid;
        border-color: black;
    }
    h2 {
        border-width: 2px;
        border-style: dotted;
        border-color: black;
    }
</style>
```

Note, in particular, that my single style rule for the h2 element gets applied to all the <h2> tags in the web page. That's the power of a style sheet: You need only a single rule to apply one or more style declarations to every instance of a particular element.

The internal style sheet method is best when you want to apply a particular set of style rules to just a single web page. If you have rules that you want applied to multiple pages, you need to go the external style sheet route.

Linking to an external style sheet

Style sheets get insanely powerful when you use an *external style sheet*, which is a separate file that contains your style rules. To use these rules within any web page, you add a special `<link>` tag inside the page head. This tag specifies the name of the external style sheet file, and the browser then uses that file to grab the style rules.

Here are the steps you need to follow to set up an external style sheet:

1. **Use your favorite text editor to create a shiny new text file.**

2. **Add your style rules to this file.**

   Note that you don't need the `<style>` tag or any other HTML tags.

3. **Save the file.**

   It's traditional to save external style sheet files using a `.css` extension (for example, `styles.css`). You can either save the file in the same folder as your HTML file, or you can create a subfolder (named, say, `css` or `styles`).

4. **For every page in which you want to use the styles, add a `<link>` tag inside the page's head section.**

   Here's the general format to use (where *filename*`.css` is the name of your external style sheet file):

   ```
   <link rel="stylesheet" href="filename.css">
   ```

   If you created a subfolder for your CSS files, be sure to add the subfolder to the `href` value (for example, `href="styles/`*filename*`.css")`.

For example, suppose you create a style sheet file named styles. css, and that file includes the following style rules:

```
h1 {
    color: blue;
}
p {
    font-size: 24px;
}
```

You then refer to that file by using the <link> tag, as shown here:

```
<!DOCTYPE html>
<html lang="en">
    <head>
        <link rel="stylesheet" href="styles.css">
    </head>
    <body>
        <h1>This Heading Will Appear Blue</h1>
        <p>This text will be displayed in a
    24-pixel font.</p>
    </body>
</html>
```

Why is this use of a style sheet so powerful? You can add the same <link> tag to any number of web pages and they'll all use the same style rules, making it a breeze to create a consistent look and feel for your site. And if you decide that your <h1> text should be green instead, all you have to do is edit the style sheet file (styles.css). Automatically, every single one of your pages that link to this file will be updated with the new style!

Chapter **2**

Constructing Pages with Good Bones

n real estate, describing a house as having *good bones* means the house has (among other attributes) a solid foundation, well-built framing, and a decent roof. In other words, the house has a strong overall structure.

When it comes to building web homes, you want your pages to have good bones, as well. Creating that solid structure is the province of HTML, particularly the elements used to convert plain text into the structural elements of the page.

In this chapter, you explore those foundational HTML tags that add the most basic structure to any page, including headings and paragraphs, articles and sections, and headers and footers. You also learn about a few other structure-related elements for creating things like line breaks and horizontal rules. What you learn in this chapter will form the basis of every web page project you undertake.

Getting to Know HTML's Basic Structure Tags

One of the most important concepts you need to understand as you get started with HTML is that whatever text you shoehorn between the `<body>` and `</body>` tags has no inherent structure. To show you what I mean, I copied the first few headings and paragraphs of this section and pasted them into an HTML file. Figure 2-1 shows what happens when I open the HTML file in a web browser.

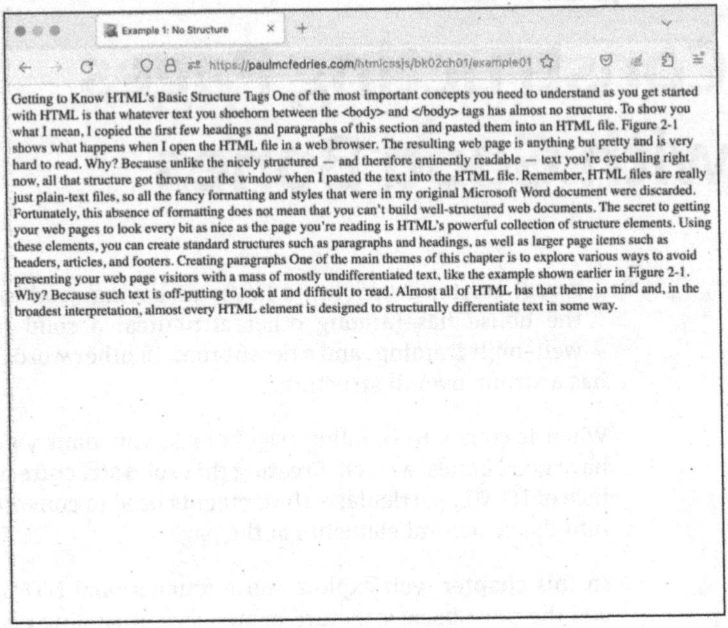

FIGURE 2-1: Bare text has no structure in an HTML document.

The resulting web page is anything but pretty and is very hard to read. Why? Because unlike the nicely structured — and therefore eminently readable — text you're eyeballing right now, all that structure got thrown out the window when I pasted the text into the HTML file. Remember, HTML files are really just plain-text files, so all the fancy formatting and styles that were in my original Microsoft Word document were discarded.

Fortunately, this absence of formatting does *not* mean that you can't build well-structured web documents. The secret to getting your web pages to look every bit as nice as the page you're reading is HTML's powerful collection of structure elements. Using these elements, you can create standard structures such as paragraphs and headings, as well as larger page items such as headers, articles, and footers.

Forging paragraphs

One of the main themes of this chapter is to explore various ways to avoid presenting your web page visitors with a mass of mostly undifferentiated text, like the example shown earlier in Figure 2-1. Why? Because such text is off-putting to look at and difficult to read.

Almost all of HTML has that theme in mind and, in the broadest interpretation, almost every HTML element is designed to structurally differentiate text in some way.

The simplest and most common example is the use of the p element, which turns any text surrounded by the <p> start tag and the </p> end tag into a paragraph:

```
<p>
    This is now a paragraph.
</p>
```

What does it mean to say that a chunk of text in a web page is a paragraph? At the most basic level, it just means that the text is rendered with a bit of space above and below. To demonstrate, I added p elements to the plain text shown earlier in Figure 2-1. The result, shown in Figure 2-2, is that the text now is separated into paragraphs, which is already a big improvement.

Getting to Know HTML's Basic Structure Tags

One of the most important concepts you need to understand as you get started with HTML is that whatever text you shoehorn between the <body> and </body> tags has almost no structure. To show you what I mean, I copied the first few headings and paragraphs of this section and pasted them into an HTML file. Figure 2-1 shows what happens when I open the HTML file in a web browser.

As you can see, the resulting web page is anything but pretty and is very hard to read. Why? Because unlike the nicely structured — and therefore eminently readable — text you're eyeballing right now, all that structure got thrown out the window when I pasted the text into the HTML file. Remember, HTML files are really just plain text files, so all the fancy formatting and styles that were in my original Microsoft Word document were discarded.

Fortunately, this does not mean that you can't build well-structured web documents. The secret to getting your web pages to look every bit as nice as the page you're reading is HTML's powerful collection of structure elements. Using these elements, you can create standard structures such as paragraphs and headings, as well as larger page items such as headers, articles, and footers.

Creating paragraphs

One of the main themes of this chapter is to explore various ways to avoid presenting your web page visitors with a mass of mostly undifferentiated text, like the example shown earlier in Figure 2-1. Why? Because such text is off-putting to look at and difficult to read.

Almost all of HTML has that theme in mind and, in the broadest interpretation, almost every HTML element is designed to structurally differentiate text in some way.

FIGURE 2-2: The text from Figure 2-1 separated into paragraphs by adding <p> tags.

Here's what the first part of the body of the HTML file now looks like:

```
Getting to Know HTML's Basic Structure Tags
<p>
     One of the most important concepts you need
     to understand as you get started with HTML is
     that whatever text you shoehorn between the
     &lt;body&gt; and &lt;/body&gt; tags has almost
     no structure. To show you what I mean, I copied
     the first few headings and paragraphs of this
     section and pasted them into an HTML file.
     Figure 2-1 shows what happens when I open the
     HTML file in a web browser.
</p>
<p>
     The resulting web page is anything but pretty
     and is very hard to read. Why? Because unlike
     the nicely structured — and therefore eminently
     readable — text you're eyeballing right now, all
```

```
that structure got thrown out the window when
I pasted the text into the HTML file. Remember,
HTML files are really just plain text files,
so all the fancy formatting and styles that were
in my original Microsoft Word document were
discarded.
</p>
```

What's with the ‹ and › gobbledygook in the first paragraph? These are examples of HTML entity names, which you use to insert special characters into your HTML code. In this case, ‹ inserts the less-than symbol (<) and › inserts the greater-than symbol (>). I needed to include these inserts because otherwise the browser would read ‹body› and ‹/body› as tags instead of text and try to interpret them as such, which would cause all kinds of problems. Check out Chapter 3 for more info on entity names.

Naming page parts with headings

In Chapter 1, I mention that you can give your web page a title using the aptly named ‹title› tag. However, that title appears only in the browser's tab. What if you want to add a title that appears in the body of the page? That's almost easier done than said because HTML comes with a few tags that enable you to define *headings*, which are bits of text that appear in a separate paragraph and usually stick out from the surrounding text by being bigger, appearing in a bold typeface, and so on.

There are six heading tags in all, ranging from <h1>, which uses the largest type size, down to <h6>, which uses the smallest size. Each of these start tags has a corresponding end tag, from ‹/h1› down to ‹/h6›.

Here's some web page code that demonstrates the six heading tags, and Figure 2-3 shows how they look in a web browser:

```
<h1>This is Heading 1</h1>
<h2>This is Heading 2</h2>
<h3>This is Heading 3</h3>
<h4>This is Heading 4</h4>
<h5>This is Heading 5</h5>
<h6>This is Heading 6</h6>
```

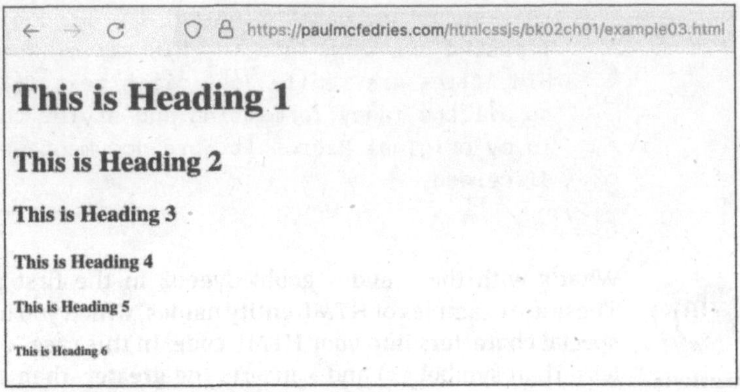

This is Heading 1

This is Heading 2

This is Heading 3

This is Heading 4

This is Heading 5

This is Heading 6

FIGURE 2-3: The six HTML heading tags.

What's up with all the different headings? The idea is that you use them to create a kind of outline for your web page. How you do this depends on the page, but here's one possibility:

>> Use <h1> for the overall page title.

>> Use <h2> for the page subtitle.

>> Use <h3> for the titles of the main sections of your page.

>> Use <h4> for the titles of the subsections of your page.

REMEMBER

Each web page you create should have only one h1 element. Technically, you're allowed to use multiple h1 elements, but it's considered a best practice to have only one.

WARNING

Don't skip heading levels. For example, if you use an h1 and then an h2, don't jump next to h4. Skipping levels like this can mess up programs that rely on a consistent use of headings to create things like a table of contents for your page.

For example, in the paragraph-enhanced web page shown earlier in Figure 2-2, the first line ("Getting to Know HTML's Basic Structure Tag") is the title of a main section, whereas the line by itself closer to the bottom ("Creating paragraphs") is the title of a subsection. I can turn these into headings, like so:

```
<h3>Getting to Know HTML's Basic Structure Tag</h3>
<h4>Creating paragraphs</h4>
```

Figure 2-4 shows the results.

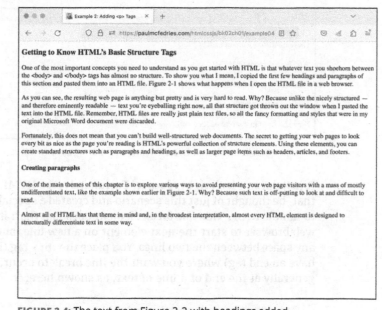

Getting to Know HTML's Basic Structure Tags

One of the most important concepts you need to understand as you get started with HTML is that whatever text you shoehorn between the <body> and </body> tags has almost no structure. To show you what I mean, I copied the first few headings and paragraphs of this section and pasted them into an HTML file. Figure 2-1 shows what happens when I open the HTML file in a web browser.

As you can see, the resulting web page is anything but pretty and is very hard to read. Why? Because unlike the nicely structured — and therefore eminently readable — text you're eyeballing right now, all that structure got thrown out the window when I pasted the text into the HTML file. Remember, HTML files are really just plain text files, so all the fancy formatting and styles that were in my original Microsoft Word document were discarded.

Fortunately, this does not mean that you can't build well-structured web pages. The secret to getting your web pages to look every bit as nice as the page you're reading is HTML's powerful collection of structure elements. Using these elements, you can create standard structures such as paragraphs and headings, as well as larger page items such as headers, articles, and footers.

Creating paragraphs

One of the main themes of this chapter is to explore various ways to avoid presenting your web page visitors with a mass of mostly undifferentiated text, like the example shown earlier in Figure 2-1. Why? Because such text is off-putting to look at and difficult to read.

Almost all of HTML has that theme in mind and, in the broadest interpretation, almost every HTML element is designed to structurally differentiate text in some way.

FIGURE 2-4: The text from Figure 2-2 with headings added.

Giving a line a break

If you look closely at the paragraphs and headings shown in Figure 2-4, one of the first things you may notice is that the browser renders the elements with a significant amount of space between them. That's a good thing, because it's that empty space that makes the page so much more readable than the all-crammed-together text from Figure 2-1.

However, with some forms of text, the "paragraphs" are single lines, such as address blocks, code listings, or poems. In these cases, you *don't* want all that white space between the lines. For example, Figure 2-5 shows what happens when I code the following limerick with <p> tags:

```
<p>There once was woman named Elle,
<p>Who learned tons of HTML.
<p>Then she came to an ode
<p>That she just couldn't code,
<p>Now she lives in a white padded cell.
```

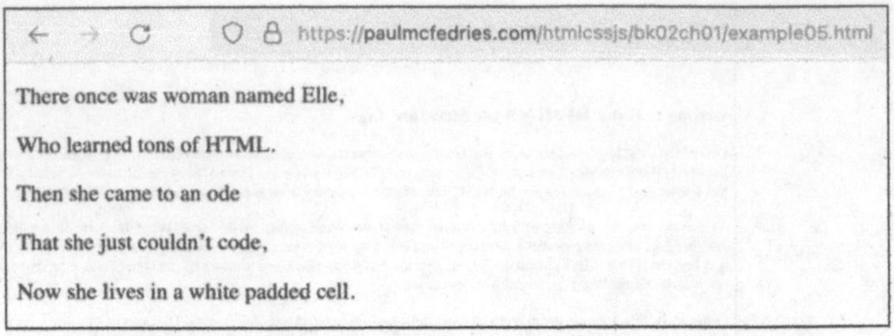

There once was woman named Elle,

Who learned tons of HTML.

Then she came to an ode

That she just couldn't code,

Now she lives in a white padded cell.

FIGURE 2-5: A limerick that has each line as a paragraph.

It just doesn't look right, does it? Fortunately, the HTML powers-that-be thought of just this scenario and created a special element to handle it: br. This *line break* element does just that: it tells the web browser to start the next element on a new line, but without any space between the two lines. You place the <br> tag (it doesn't have an end tag) where you want the line break to occur, which is generally at the end of a line of text, as shown here:

```
There once was woman named Elle,<br>
Who learned tons of HTML.<br>
Then she came to an ode<br>
That she just couldn't code,<br>
Now she lives in a white padded cell.
```

Figure 2-6 shows the result. Ah, that's better!

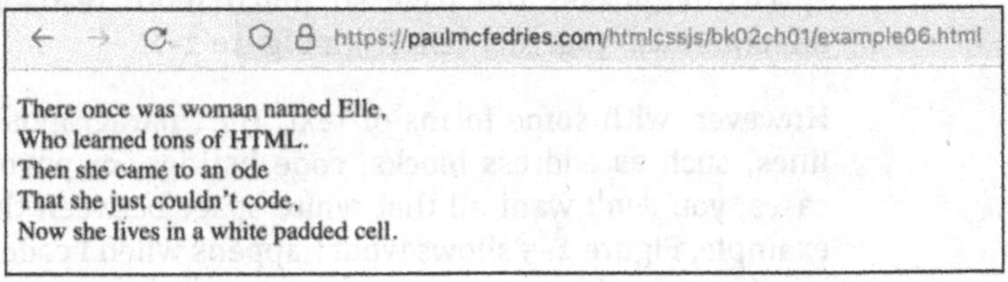

There once was woman named Elle,
Who learned tons of HTML.
Then she came to an ode
That she just couldn't code,
Now she lives in a white padded cell.

FIGURE 2-6: The limerick using line breaks instead of paragraphs.

Now it's time to take these page-structure ramblings to the next level with an in-depth look at HTML's so-called *semantic* page elements. After you've mastered the tags I cover in the next section, you'll know everything you need to know to build pages with good digital bones.

Structuring the Page

Your web pages will be messy and unreadable unless you add some structure to the body section. I talk about structural elements such as headings and paragraphs earlier in this chapter, but now I'm kicking things up a notch and talking about HTML's high-level structure tags.

The first thing to understand about these tags is that they're designed to infuse meaning — that is, semantics — into your page structures. You'll learn what this means as I introduce each tag, but for now, get a load of the abstract page shown in Figure 2-7.

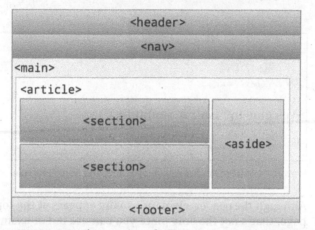

FIGURE 2-7: An abstract view of HTML's semantic page structure tags.

The following sections take a look at each of the tags shown in Figure 2-7.

The <header> tag

You use the <header> tag to create a *page header*, which is usually a strip across the top of the page that includes elements such as the site or page title and a logo. (Don't confuse this with the page's head section that appears between the <head> and </head> tags.)

Because the header almost always appears at the top of the page, the ⟨header⟩ tag is usually seen right after the ⟨body⟩ tag, as shown in the following example (and Figure 2-8):

```
<body>
    <header>
        <img src="iis-logo.png" alt="Isn't it
    Semantic? company logo">
            <h1>Welcome to "Isn't it Semantic?"</h1>
            <hr>
    </header>
    ...
</body>
```

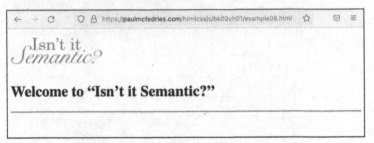

FIGURE 2-8: A page header with a logo, title, and horizontal rule.

REMEMBER

Although the header element usually appears at the top of a web page, that's not the only place you can use it. For example, if you have section elements that begin with introductory content — for example, an icon, a section number, a link, or a date — you can add a header element at the beginning of each section.

The ⟨nav⟩ tag

The ⟨nav⟩ tag defines a page section that includes a few elements that help visitors navigate your site. These elements could be links to the main sections of the site, links (check out Chapter 3) to recently posted content, or a search feature. The ⟨nav⟩ section typically appears near the top of the page, just after the header, as shown here (and in Figure 2-9):

```
<body>
    <header>
        <img src="iis-logo.png" alt="Isn't it
Semantic? company logo">
        <h1>Welcome to "Isn't it Semantic?"</h1>
        <hr>
    </header>
    <nav>
        <a href="/">Home</a>
        <a href="semantics.html">Semantics</a>
        <a href="contact.html">Contact</a>
        <a href="about.html">About</a>
    </nav>
    . . .
</body>
```

https://paulmcfedries.com/htmlcssjs/bk02ch01/example09.html

Isn't it
Semantic?

Welcome to "Isn't it Semantic?"

Home Semantics Contact About

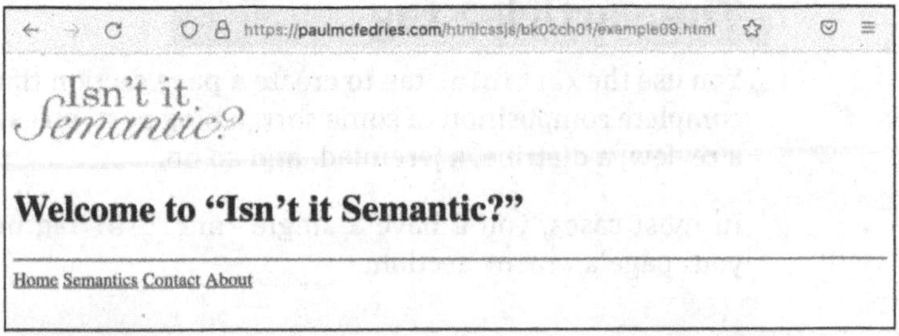

FIGURE 2-9: The <nav> section usually appears just after the <header> section.

REMEMBER

Feel free to use the nav element anywhere you have navigational links. Sitewide navigational links are almost always tucked into a nav element that appears just below the main page header. However, you may have navigational links specific to an article or section, and it's perfectly fine to put a nav element near the top of those elements.

The <main> tag

The <main> tag sets up a section to hold the content that is, in a sense, the point of the page. For example, if you're creating the page to tell everyone all that you know about Siamese Fighting Fish, your Siamese Fighting Fish text, images, links, and so on would go into the <main> section.

The `<main>` section usually comes right after the `<head>` and `<nav>` sections:

```
<body>
    <header>
    . . .
    </header>
    <nav>
    . . .
    </nav>
    <main>
        Main content goes here
    </main>
    . . .
</body>
```

The <article> tag

You use the `<article>` tag to create a page section that contains a complete composition of some sort: a blog post, an essay, a poem, a review, a diatribe, a jeremiad, and so on.

In most cases, you'll have a single `<article>` tag nested inside your page's `<main>` section:

```
<body>
    <header>
        . . .
    </header>
    <nav>
        . . .
    </nav>
    <main>
        <article>
            Article content goes here
        </article>
    </main>
    . . .
</body>
```

However, it isn't a hard and fast rule that your page can have only one <article> tag. In fact, it isn't a rule at all. If you want to have two compositions in your page — and thus two <article> sections within your <main> tag — be my guest.

The <section> tag

The <section> tag indicates a major part of page: usually a heading tag followed by some text. How do you know whether a chunk of the page is "major" or not? The easiest way is to imagine if your page had a table of contents. If you'd want a particular part of your page to be included in that table of contents, it's major enough to merit the <section> tag.

Most of the time, your <section> tags will appear within an <article> tag:

```
<main>
    <article>
<section>
            Section 1 heading goes here
            Section 1 text goes here
        </section>
<section>
            Section 2 heading goes here
            Section 2 text goes here
        </section>
        ...
    </article>
</main>
```

The <aside> tag

You use the <aside> tag to cordon off a bit of the page for content that, although important or relevant for the site as a whole, is at best tangentially related to the page's <main> content. The <aside> is often a sidebar that includes site news or links to recent content, but it may also include links to other site pages that are related to current page.

The `<aside>` element most often appears within the `<main>` area, but after the `<article>` content.

```
<body>
    <header>
        ...
    </header>
    <nav>
        ...
    </nav>
    <main>
        <article>
            ...
        </article>
        <aside>
            Aside content goes here
        </aside>
    </main>
    ...
</body>
```

The <footer> tag

You use the `<footer>` tag to create a *page footer*, which is typically a strip across the bottom of the page that includes elements such as a copyright notice, contact info, and social media links.

Because the footer almost always appears at the bottom of the page, the `<footer>` tag is usually seen right before the `</body>` end tag, as shown here:

```
<body>
    <header>
        ...
    </header>
    <nav>
        ...
    </nav>
    <main>
        <article>
            ...
        </article>
```

```
        <aside>
          ...
        </aside>
      </main>
      <footer>
          Footer content goes here
      </footer>
    </body>
```

Handling non-semantic content with <div>

The <header>, <nav>, <main>, <article>, <section>, <aside>, and <footer> elements create meaningful structures within your page, which is why HTML nerds call these *semantic* elements. Even the humble <p> tag introduced earlier in this chapter is semantic in that it represents a single paragraph, usually within a <section> element.

But what's a would-be web weaver to do when they want to add a chunk of content that just doesn't fit any of the standard semantic tags? That happens a lot, and the solution is to slap that content inside a div (for "division") element. The <div> tag is a generic container that doesn't represent anything meaningful, so it's the perfect place for any non-semantic stuff that needs a home:

```
<div>
    Non-semantic content goes right here
</div>
```

Here's an example:

```
<div>
    Requisite social media links:
</div>
<div>
    <a href="https://facebook.com/">Facebook</a>
    <a href="https://twitter.com/">Twitter</a>
    <a href="https://instagram.com/">Instagram</a>
    <a href="http://www.hbo.com/silicon-valley">
  Hooli</a>
</div>
```

Notice in Figure 2-10 that the browser renders the two `<div>` elements on separate lines.

← → C   ○ 🔒 https://paulmcfedries.com/htmlcssjs/bk02ch01/example10.html

Requisite social media links:
Facebook Twitter Instagram Hooli

FIGURE 2-10: The browser renders each `<div>` section on a new line.

Handling words and characters with <span>

If you want to do something with a small chunk of a larger piece of text, such as a phrase, a word, or even a character or three, you need to turn to a so-called *inline element*, which creates a container that exists within some larger element and flows along with the rest of the content in that larger element. The most common inline element to use is `<span>`, which creates a container around a bit of text:

```
<p>
Notice how an <span style="font-variant: small-
   caps">
inline element</span> flows right along with the
rest of the text.
</p>
```

What's happening here is that the `<span>` tag is applying a style called *small caps* to the text between `<span>` and `</span>` (`inline element`). As shown in Figure 2-11, the `<span>` text flows along with the rest of the paragraph.

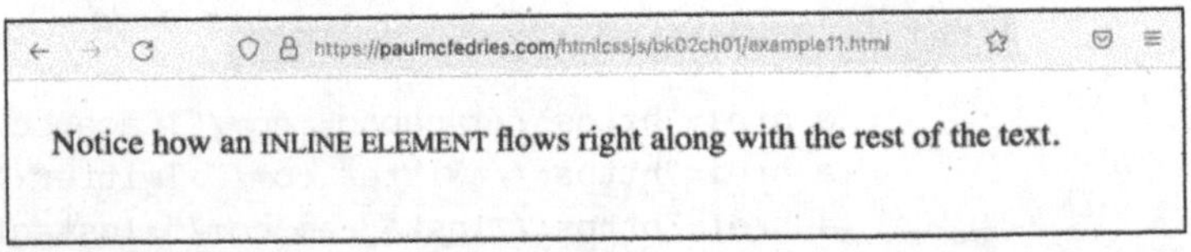

← → C   ○ 🔒 https://paulmcfedries.com/htmlcssjs/bk02ch01/example11.html   ☆   ♡ ☰

Notice how an INLINE ELEMENT flows right along with the rest of the text.

FIGURE 2-11: Using `<span>` makes the container flow with the surrounding text.

IN THIS CHAPTER

» **Marking emphasized and important text**

» **Dealing with quotations**

» **Adding links to your page**

» **Building bulleted and numbered lists**

» **Sprucing up your pages with images**

Chapter **3**
Adding Links, Lists, and Images

I n this chapter, you investigate many of HTML's text-related tags. For example, you learn the elements that mark up text that you want emphasized in some way. You find out how to add quotations and how to turn any chunk of text into a link. You also explore the wonderful world of HTML list-making, which includes building both bulleted and numbered lists. Do you need to add characters such as © (copyright) and € (euro) to your pages? You learn how to add those and many other special symbols. Finally, I close the chapter with a quick look at how to add images to your pages.

Applying the Basic Text Tags

HTML has a few tags that enable you to add structure to text. Many web developers use these tags only for the built-in browser formatting that comes with them, but you really should try to use the tags *semantically*, as the geeks say, which means to use them based on the meaning you want the text to convey.

Emphasizing text

One of the most common meanings you can attach to text is emphasis. By putting a little extra oomph on a word or phrase, you tell the reader to add stress to that text, which can subtly alter the meaning of your words. For example, consider the following sentence:

```
You'll never fit in there with that ridiculous
    thing on your head!
```

Now consider the same sentence with emphasis added to one word:

```
You'll never fit in there with that ridiculous
    thing on your head!
```

You emphasize text on a web page by surrounding that text with the <em> and </em> tags:

```
You'll <em>never</em> fit in there with that
    ridiculous thing on your head!
```

All web browsers render the emphasized text in italics, as shown in Figure 3-1.

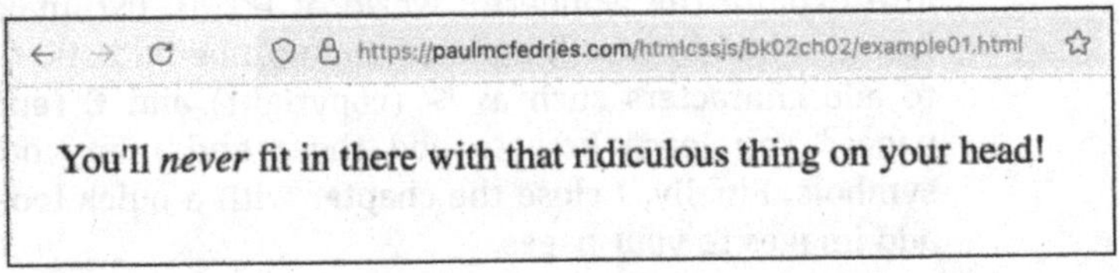

https://paulmcfedries.com/htmlcssjs/bk02ch02/example01.html

You'll *never* fit in there with that ridiculous thing on your head!

FIGURE 3-1: The web browser renders emphasized text using italics.

I should also mention that HTML has a closely related tag: <i>. The <i> tag's job is to mark up *alternative text*, which refers to any text that you want treated with a different mood or role than regular text. Common examples include book titles, technical terms, foreign words, or a person's thoughts. All web browsers render text between <i> and </i> in italics.

Marking important text

One common meaning that you'll often want your text to convey is importance. It may be some significant step in a procedure, a vital prerequisite or condition for something, or a crucial passage within a longer text block. In each case, you're dealing with text that you don't want your readers to miss, so it needs to stand out from the regular prose that surrounds it. In HTML, you mark text as important by surrounding it with the <strong> and </strong> tags, as in this example:

```
Dear reader: Do you see the red button in the
upper-right corner of this page? <strong>Never
click the red button!</strong> You have been
warned.
```

All web browsers render text marked up with the <strong> tag in bold, as shown in Figure 3-2.

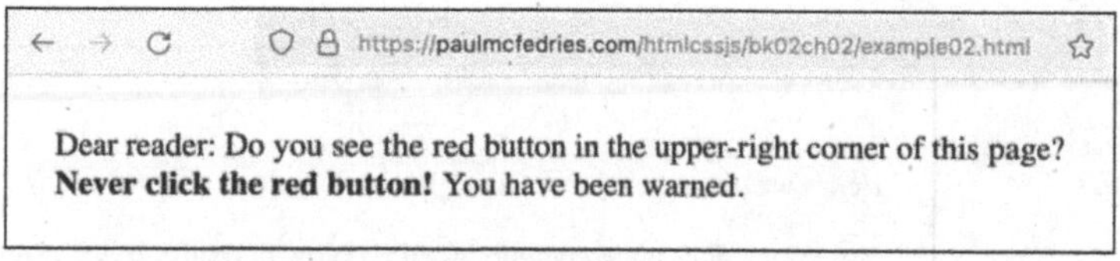

Dear reader: Do you see the red button in the upper-right corner of this page? **Never click the red button!** You have been warned.

FIGURE 3-2: The browser renders important text using bold.

Just to keep us all on our web development toes, HTML also offers a close cousin of the <strong> tag: the <b> tag. You use the <b> tag to mark up keywords in the text. A *keyword* is a term that you want to draw attention to because it plays a different role than the regular text. It could be a company name or a person's name (think of those famous "bold-faced names" that are the staple of celebrity gossip columns). The browser renders text between the <b> and </b> tags in a bold font.

Adding quotations

The readers of your web pages may be quote appreciators, so why not sprinkle your text with a few words from the wise? In

HTML, you designate a passage of text as a quotation by using the `<blockquote>` tag. Here's an example:

```
Here's what the great jurist Oliver Wendell
    Holmes, Sr. had to say about puns:
<blockquote>
A pun does not commonly justify a blow in return.
    But if a blow were given for such cause, and
    death ensued, the jury would be judges both of
    the facts and of the pun, and might, if the
    latter were of an aggravated character, return a
    verdict of justifiable homicide.
</blockquote>
Clearly, the dude was not a pun fan.
```

The web browser renders the text between `<blockquote>` and `</blockquote>` in its own paragraph that it also indents slightly from the left margin, as shown in Figure 3-3.

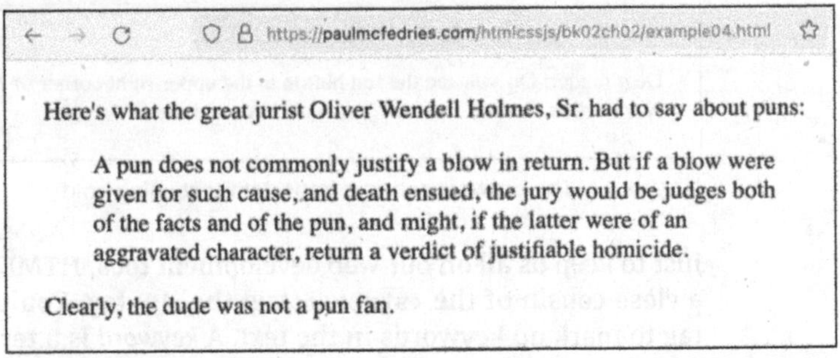

FIGURE 3-3: The web browser renders `<blockquote>` text indented slighted from the left.

I should also mention the closely related q element, which you can use to mark up a so-called *inline quotation*. You use an inline quotation for short quotes that can flow along with the regular text. Here's an example:

```
Whether you love or hate people who pun, you can't
    argue with Ron Wolfe, who said that <q>A punster
    is someone who shticks by his word.</q>
```

As shown in Figure 3-4, the web browser renders the quote between quotation marks.

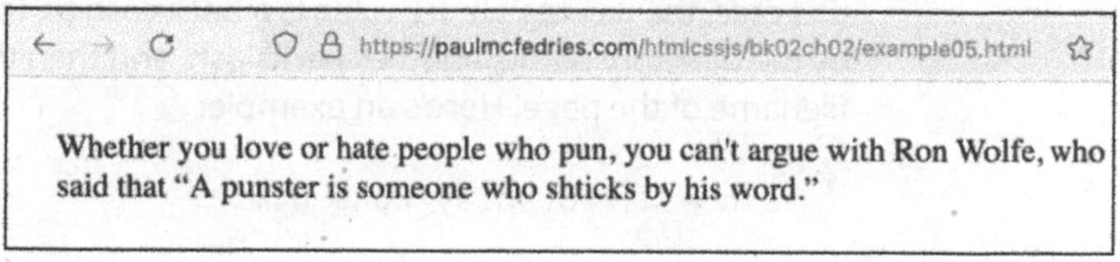

> ← → C   ○ 🔒 https://paulmcfedries.com/htmlcssjs/bk02ch02/example05.html   ☆
>
> Whether you love or hate people who pun, you can't argue with Ron Wolfe, who said that "A punster is someone who shticks by his word."

FIGURE 3-4: The web browser renders `<q>` text surrounded by quotation marks.

Creating Links

The HTML tags that do the link thing are `<a>` and `</a>`. Here's how the `<a>` tag works:

```
<a href="address">
```

Here, `href` stands for *hypertext reference*, which is just a fancy-schmancy way of saying "address" or "URL." Your job is to replace *address* with the actual address of the web page you want to use for the link. And yes, you have to enclose the address in quotation marks. The form of `address` value you use depends on where the web page is located with respect to the page that has the link. There are three possibilities:

» **Remote web page:** Refers to a web page that's not part of your website. In this case, the `<a>` tag's `href` value is the full URL of the page. Here's an example:

```
<a href="https://webdev.mcfedries.com/wb">
```

» **Local web page in the same directory:** Refers to a web page that's part of your website and is stored in the same directory as the HTML file that has the link. In this case, the `<a>` tag's `href` value is the filename of the page. Here's an example:

```
<a href="rutabagas.html">
```

>> **Local web page in a different directory:** Refers to a web page that's part of your website and is stored in a directory other than the one used by the HTML file that has the link. In this case, the `<a>` tag's `href` value is a backslash (/), followed by the directory name, another backslash, and then the filename of the page. Here's an example:

```
<a href="/wordplay/puns.html">
```

You're not done yet, though, not by a long shot (insert groan of disappointment here). What are you missing? Right: You have to give the reader some descriptive link text to click. That's pretty straightforward because all you do is insert the text between the `<a>` and `</a>` tags, like this:

```
<a href="address">Link text</a>
```

Need an example? You got it:

```
To play with HTML and CSS, check out the
<a href="https://webdevworkshop.io/wb">
Web Dev Workbench</a>!
```

Figure 3-5 shows how it looks in a web browser. Notice how the browser colors and underlines the link text, and when I point my mouse at the link, the address I specified in the `<a>` tag appears in the lower-left corner of the browser window.

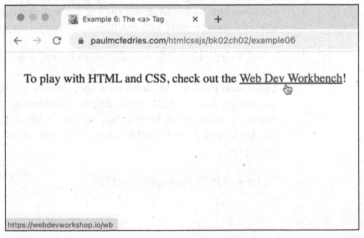

FIGURE 3-5: How the link appears in the web browser.

Building Bulleted and Numbered Lists

HTML has a few tags that are specially designed to give you control over your list-building chores. For example, you can create a bulleted list that actually has those little bullets out front of each item. Nice! Want a Top Ten list, instead? HTML has your back by offering special tags for numbered lists, too.

Making your point with bulleted lists

A no-frills, `<br>`-separated list isn't very useful or readable because it doesn't come with any type of eye candy that helps differentiate one item from the next. An official, HTML-approved bulleted list solves that problem by leading off each item with a bullet — a cute little black dot. Bulleted lists use two types of tags:

>> The entire list is surrounded by the `<ul>` and `</ul>` tags. Why "ul"? Well, what the rest of the world calls a bulleted list, the HTML poohbahs call an *unordered list.*

>> Each item in the list is preceded by the `<li>` (list item) tag and is closed with the `</li>` end tag. (Technically, the `</li>` end tag is optional as long as the next item is either another `<li>` tag or the `</ul>` end tag.)

The general setup looks like this:

```
<ul>
    <li>Bullet text goes here</li>
    <li>And here</li>
    <li>And here</li>
    <li>You get the idea...</li>
</ul>
```

Notice that I've indented the list items by four spaces, which makes it easier to realize that they're part of a `<ul></ul>` container. Here's an example to chew on:

```
<h3>My All-Time Favorite Oxymorons</h3>
<ul>
    <li>Pretty ugly</li>
    <li>Military intelligence</li>
    <li>Jumbo shrimp</li>
```

```
    <li>Original copy</li>
    <li>Random order</li>
    <li>Act naturally</li>
    <li>Tight slacks</li>
    <li>Freezer burn</li>
    <li>Sight unseen</li>
    <li>Microsoft Works</li>
</ul>
```

Figure 3-6 shows how the web browser renders this code, cute little bullets and all.

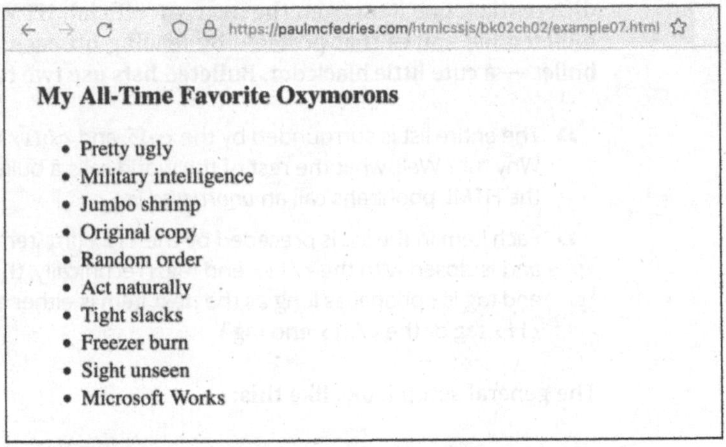

← → C   ○ 🔒 https://paulmcfedries.com/htmlcssjs/bk02ch02/example07.html ☆

My All-Time Favorite Oxymorons

- Pretty ugly
- Military intelligence
- Jumbo shrimp
- Original copy
- Random order
- Act naturally
- Tight slacks
- Freezer burn
- Sight unseen
- Microsoft Works

FIGURE 3-6: A typical bulleted list.

TIP

If your unordered list of items consists of commands that a page visitor can run, then a semantic alternative to ul is the menu element, which represents an unordered list of commands. You build your menu list in exactly the same way as a ul list. That is, your commands are each surrounded by <li> and </li> tags, and all of those are surrounded by <menu> and </menu>:

```
<menu>
    <li>Settings</li>
    <li>Account</li>
    <li>Help</li>
</menu>
```

Numbered lists: Easy as one, two, three

If you want to include a numbered list of items — it could be a Top Ten list, bowling league standings, steps to follow, or any kind of ranking — don't bother inserting the numbers yourself. Instead, you can use an HTML *numbered list* to make the web browser generate the numbers for you. As do bulleted lists, numbered lists use two types of tags:

» The entire list is surrounded by the <ol> and </ol> tags. The "ol" here is short for *ordered list,* because those HTML nerds just have to be different, don't they?

» Each item in the list is surrounded by <li> and </li>.

Here's the general structure to use:

```
<ol>
    <li>First item</li>
    <li>Second item</li>
    <li>Third item</li>
    <li>You got this....</li>
</ol>
```

I've indented the list items by four spaces to make it easier to notice that they're inside an <ol></ol> container. Here's an example:

```
<h3>My Ten Favorite U.S. College Nicknames</h3>
<ol>
    <li>U.C. Santa Cruz Banana Slugs</li>
    <li>Delta State Fighting Okra</li>
    <li>Kent State Golden Flashes</li>
    <li>Evergreen State College Geoducks</li>
    <li>New Mexico Tech Pygmies</li>
    <li>South Carolina Fighting Gamecocks</li>
    <li>Southern Illinois Salukis</li>
    <li>Whittier Poets</li>
    <li>Western Illinois Leathernecks</li>
    <li>Delaware Fightin' Blue Hens</li>
</ol>
```

Notice that I didn't include any numbers before each list item. However, when I display this document in a browser (check out Figure 3-7), the numbers are automatically inserted. Pretty slick, huh?

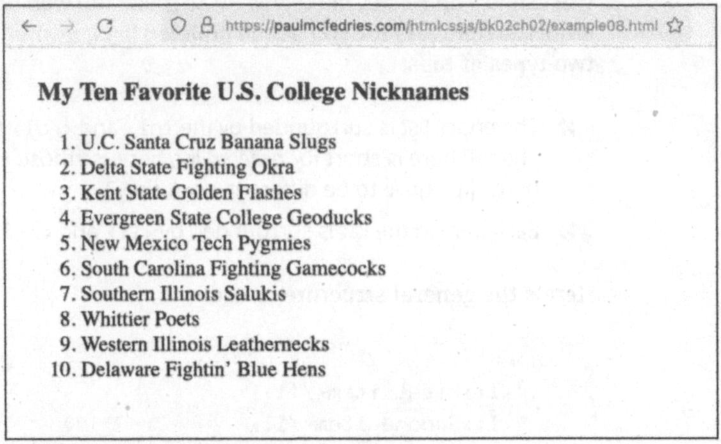

← → C   ○ 🔒 https://paulmcfedries.com/htmlcssjs/bk02ch02/example08.html ☆

My Ten Favorite U.S. College Nicknames

1. U.C. Santa Cruz Banana Slugs
2. Delta State Fighting Okra
3. Kent State Golden Flashes
4. Evergreen State College Geoducks
5. New Mexico Tech Pygmies
6. South Carolina Fighting Gamecocks
7. Southern Illinois Salukis
8. Whittier Poets
9. Western Illinois Leathernecks
10. Delaware Fightin' Blue Hens

FIGURE 3-7: When the web browser renders the ordered list, it's kind enough to add the numbers for you automatically.

Inserting Special Characters

In Chapter 1, I talk briefly about a special ‹meta› tag that goes into the head section:

```
<meta charset="utf-8">
```

It may not look like it, but that tag adds a bit of magic to your web page. The voodoo is that now you can add special characters such as © and ™ directly to your web page text, and the web browser will display them without complaint. The trick is how you add these characters directly to your text, and that depends on your operating system. First, if you're using Windows, you have two choices:

>> Hold down the Alt key and then press the character's four-digit ASCII code using your keyboard's numeric keypad. For example, you type an em dash (—) by pressing Alt+0151.

>> Paste the character from the Character Map application that comes with Windows.

If you're a Mac user, you also have two choices:

» Type the character's special keyboard shortcut. For example, you type an em dash (—) by pressing Option+Shift+- (hyphen).

» Paste the character from the Symbols Viewer that comes with macOS.

Having said all that, I should point out that there's another way to add special characters to a page. The web wizards who created HTML came up with special codes called *character entities* (which is surely a name only a true geek would love) that represent these oddball symbols. These codes come in two flavors: a *character reference* and an *entity name*. Character references are basically just numbers, and the entity names are friendlier symbols that describe the character you're trying to display. For example, you can display the registered trademark symbol (™) by using either the ® character reference or the ® entity name, as shown here:

```
Print-On-Non-Demand&#174;
```

or

```
Print-On-Non-Demand&reg;
```

Note that both character references and entity names begin with an ampersand (&) and end with a semicolon (;). Don't forget either character when using special symbols in your own pages.

REMEMBER

One very common use of character references is for displaying HTML tags without the web browser rendering them as tags. To do this, replace the tag's less-than sign (<) with < (or <) and the tag's greater-than sign (>) with > (or >).

Inserting Images

Whether you want to tell stories, give instructions, pontificate, or just plain rant about something, you can do all that and more by adding text to your page. But to make it more interesting for your readers, add a bit of imagery every now and then. To that end, there's an HTML tag you can use to add one or more images to your page.

First, a mercifully brief look at image formats

Before getting too far into this picture business, I should tell you that, unfortunately, you can't use just any old image on a web page. Browsers are limited in the types of images they can display. There are, in fact, four main types of image formats you can use:

>> **GIF:** The original web graphics format (it's short for Graphics Interchange Format). GIF (pronounced "giff" or "jiff") is limited to 256 colors, so it's rarely used for static images. Instead, most folks nowadays use animated GIFs, which combine multiple image files into a single animation.

TIP

Want to create your own animated GIFs? Of course you do! The easiest way is to use one of the online sites that offer this service. Two popular sites are GIPHY (https://giphy.com/create/gifmaker) and Canva (www.canva.com/create/gif-maker).

>> **JPEG:** Gets its name from the Joint Photographic Experts Group that invented it. JPEG (it's pronounced "jay-peg") supports complex images that have many millions of colors. The main advantage of JPEG files is that, given the same image, they're smaller than GIFs, so they take less time to download. Careful, though: JPEG uses *lossy* compression, which means that it makes the image smaller by discarding redundant pixels. The greater the compression, the more pixels that are discarded, and the less sharp the image will appear. That said, if you have a photo or similarly complex image, JPEG is almost always the best choice because it gives the smallest file size.

>> **PNG:** The Portable Network Graphics format supports millions of colors. PNG (pronounced "p-n-g" or "ping") is a compressed format, but unlike JPEGs, PNGs use *lossless* compression. This means that images retain sharpness, but the file sizes can get quite big. If you have an illustration or icon that uses solid colors, or a photo that contains large areas of near-solid color, PNG is a good choice. PNG also supports transparency.

>> **SVG:** With the Scalable Vector Graphics format, images are generated using *vectors* (mathematical formulas based on

points and shapes on a grid) rather than pixels. Surprisingly, these vectors reside as a set of instructions in a special-text-based format, which means you can edit the image using a text editor! SVG is a good choice for illustrations, particularly if you have software that supports the SVG format, such as Inkscape or Adobe Illustrator.

Inserting an image

Okay, enough of all that. It's time to start squeezing some images onto your web page. As mentioned earlier, there's an HTML code that tells a browser to display an image. It's the <img> tag, and here's how it works:

```
<img src="filename" alt="description" title="title">
```

Here, src is short for source; *filename* is the name (and often also the location) of the graphics file you want to display; *description* is a short description of the image (which is read by screen readers and seen by users who aren't displaying images or if the image fails to load); and *title* is a tooltip that appears when the user hovers the mouse pointer over the image. Note that there's no end tag to add here.

If you use images that are purely ornamental, you don't need to describe them. In each such case, include the alt attribute in the <img> tag, but set its value to the null string (" "), like so:

```
<img src="filename" alt="" title="title">
```

Here's an example to eyeball. Suppose you have an image named logo.png. To add it to your page, you use the following line:

```
<img src="logo.png" alt="The Logophilia Ltd.
    company logo" title="Logophilia Ltd.">
```

For this simple example to work, bear in mind that your HTML file and your graphics file need to be sitting in the same directory. Many webmasters create a subdirectory just for images, which keeps things neat and tidy.

Here's an example of including an image in a web page, and Figure 3-8 shows how things appear in a web browser:

```
To see a World in a Grain of Sand<br>
And a Heaven in a Wild Flower<br>
—William Blake<br>
<img src="images/flower-and-ant.jpg" alt="Macro
    photo showing an ant exploring a flower"
    title="Flower and Ant">
```

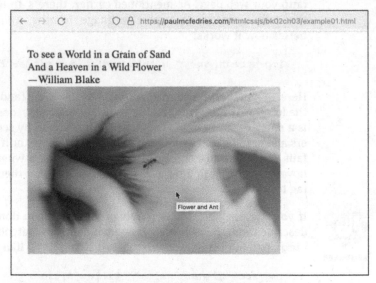

FIGURE 3-8: A web page with an image thrown in.

Turning an image into a link

Your links don't always have to be text. If you have a logo, icon, or other picture that you want your readers to click to go to a different page, you can set up that image as a link.

Here's the general technique to use:

```
<a href="address"><img src="filename" alt=
    "description"></a>
```

You set up the ‹a› tag in the usual way, but this time between ‹a› and ‹/a› you use an ‹img› tag instead of some text. Just like that, your image becomes a link that folks can click to jump to whatever page you specify in the href attribute.

Here's an example:

```
<header>
    <a href="/"><img src="images/iis-logo.png"
    alt="Isn't it Semantic? company logo"></a>
    <h1>Welcome to "Isn't it Semantic?"</h1>
    <hr>
</header>
```

Chapter **4**

Building Web Forms

HTML offers a mechanism for turning a just-sitting-there web page into an interactive one: a web form. In this chapter, you explore all that web forms have to offer. After mastering the basics, you investigate the amazing features offered by HTML web forms, which can include not only standard knickknacks such as buttons, text boxes, and lists, but also more advanced controls for selecting things like dates and colors. It's a veritable forms smorgasbord, so get ready to tuck in!

What the Heck Is a Web Form?

A form is essentially the web page equivalent of a dialog box. It's a page section populated with text boxes, lists, checkboxes, command buttons, and other controls to get information from the user.

A web form is a little data-gathering machine. What kinds of data can it gather? You name it:

>> Text, from a single word up to a long post

>> Numbers, dates, and times

>> Which item is (or items are) selected in a list

>> Whether a checkbox is selected

>> Which one of a group of radio buttons is selected

You build web forms with your bare hands using special tags. HTML includes many useful form goodies, which I show you over the next few sections.

Getting Your Form off the Ground

To get your form started, you wrap everything inside the `<form>` tag:

```
<form>
</form>
```

Including a Button

Most forms include a button that the user clicks when they've completed the form and wants to initiate the form's underlying action. This is known as *submitting* the form, and that term has traditionally meant sending the form data to a server-side script for processing. These days, however, "submitting" the form can also mean updating something on the web page without sending anything to the server. For example, clicking a button may set the page's background color.

To create a button to submit the form, use the `<button>` tag:

```
<button type="submit">buttonText</button>
```

The *buttonText* here stands in for the text that appears on the button face.

For example:

```
<button type="submit">Ship It</button>
```

For better-looking buttons, use CSS to style the following:

>> **Rounded corners:** To control the roundness of the button corners, use the `border-radius` property set to either a measurement (in, say, pixels) or a percentage. For example:

```
button {
    border-radius: 15px;
}
```

>> **Drop shadow:** To add a drop shadow to a button, apply the `box-shadow: x y blur color` property, where *x* is the horizontal offset of the shadow, *y* is the vertical offset of the shadow, *blur* is the amount the shadow is blurred, and *color* is the shadow color. For example:

```
button {
    box-shadow: 3px 3px 5px grey;
}
```

Gathering Text

When your form needs to gather some text, you can use either a text box or a text area. You can also use a label to display text on the form. I take you through all three text types in the next three sections.

Working with text boxes

Text-based fields are the most commonly used form elements, and most of them use the `<input>` tag:

```
<input type="textType" name="textName"
    value="textValue" placeholder="textPrompt">
```

The various parts of this code are as follows:

>> *textType:* The kind of text field you want to use in your form.

>> *textName:* The name you assign to the field.

>> *textValue:* The initial value of the field, if any.

>> *textPrompt:* Text that appears temporarily in the field when the page first loads and is used to prompt the user about the required input. The placeholder text disappears as soon as the user starts typing in the field.

Here's a list of the available text-based types you can use for the `type` attribute:

>> `text`: Displays a text box into which the user types a line of text. Add the `size` attribute to specify the width of the field, in characters (the default is 20). Here's an example:

```
<input type="text" name="company" size="50">
```

>> `number`: Displays a text box into which the user types a numeric value. Most browsers add a spin box that enables the user to increment or decrement the number by clicking the up or down arrow, respectively. Check out this example:

```
<input type="number" name="points" value="100">
```

I should also mention the `range` type, which displays a slider control that enables the user to click and drag to choose a numeric value between a specified minimum and maximum:

```
<input type="range" name="transparency"
    min="0" max="100" value="100">
```

>> `email`: Displays a text box into which the user types an email address. Add the `multiple` attribute to allow the user to type two or more addresses, separated by commas. Add the `size` attribute to specify the width of the field, in characters. An example for you:

```
<input type="email" name="user-email"
    placeholder="you@yourdomain.com">
```

>> `url`: Displays a text box into which the user types a URL. Add the `size` attribute to specify the width of the field, in characters. Here's a for instance:

```
<input type="url" name="homepage"
    placeholder="e.g., https://domain.com/">
```

>> `tel`: Displays a text box into which the user types a telephone number. Use the `size` attribute to specify the width of the field, in characters. Here's an example:

```
<input type="tel" name="mobile" placeholder="
   (xxx)xxx-xxxx">
```

>> `time`: Displays a text box into which the user types a time, usually hours and minutes. For example:

```
<input type="time" name="start-time">
```

>> `password`: Displays a text box into which the user types a password. The typed characters appear as dots (·). Add the `autocomplete` attribute to specify whether the user's browser or password management software can automatically enter the password. Set the attribute to `current-password` to allow password autocompletion, or to `off` to disallow autocompletion. Need an example? Done:

```
<input type="password" name="userpassword"
   autocomplete="current-password">
```

>> `search`: Displays a text box into which the user types a search term. Add the `size` attribute to specify the width of the field, in characters. Why, yes, I do have an example:

```
<input type="search" name="q" placeholder=
   "Type a search term">
```

>> `hidden`: Adds an input field to the form, but doesn't display the field to the user. That sounds weird, I know, but it's a handy way to store a value that you want to include in the submit, but you don't want the user to notice or modify. Here's an example:

```
<input id="userSession" name="user-session"
   type="hidden" value="jwr274">
```

REMEMBER

Some older browsers don't get special text fields such as `email` and `time`, but you can still use them in your pages because those clueless browsers will ignore the `type` attribute and just display a standard `text` field.

Figure 4-1 demonstrates each of these text fields, as well as the text area and the label, which I discuss in the next two sections.

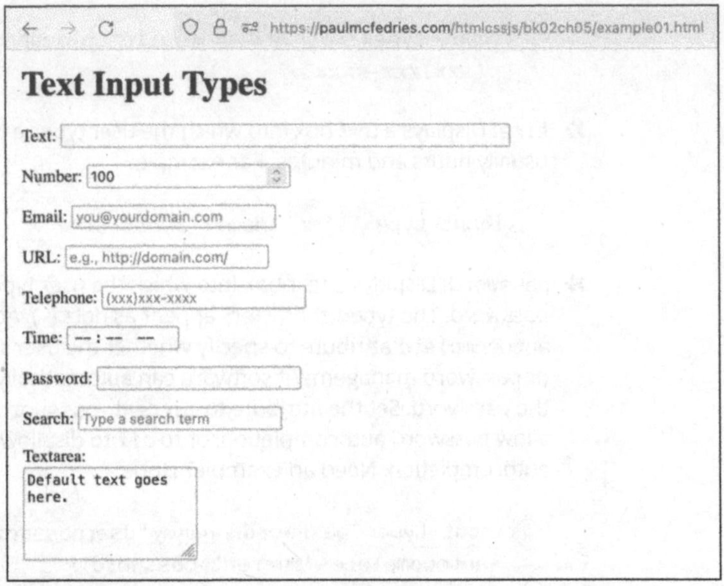

FIGURE 4-1: The various text input types you can use in your forms.

Working with text areas

The ‹textarea› tag displays a text box into which the user can type multiple lines of text. Add the rows attribute to specify how many lines of text are displayed. If you want default text to appear in the text box, add the text between the ‹textarea› and ‹/textarea› tags. Here's an example:

```
<textarea name="message" rows="5">
Default text goes here.
</textarea>
```

Adding labels

The ‹label› tag associates a label with a form field. There are two ways to use a label:

>> Method #1: Surround the form field with `<label>` and `</label>` tags, and insert the label text before or after the field, like so:

```
<label>
Email:
<input type="email" name="user-email"
   placeholder="you@yourdomain.com">
</label>
```

>> Method #2: Add an id value to the field's tag, set the `<label>` tag's for attribute to the same value, and insert the label text between the `<label>` and `</label>` tags, as I've done here:

```
<label for="useremail">Email:</label>
<input id="useremail" type="email" name="user-
   email" placeholder="you@yourdomain.com">
```

Including Checkboxes

You use a checkbox in a web form to toggle a setting on (that is, the checkbox is selected) and off (the checkbox is deselected). You create a checkbox by including in your form the following version of the `<input>` tag:

```
<input type="checkbox" name="checkName"
   value="checkValue" [checked]>
```

The various parts of this code are as follows:

>> *checkName:* The name you want to assign to the checkbox.

>> *checkValue:* The value you want to assign to the checkbox.

>> checked: When this optional attribute is present, the checkbox is initially selected.

Here's an example:

```
<fieldset>
  <legend>
      What's your phobia? (Please check all that
  apply):
  </legend>
  <label>
      <input type="checkbox" name="phobia"
value="Ants">Myrmecophobia (Fear of ants)
  </label>
  <label>
      <input type="checkbox" name="phobia"
value="Bald">Peladophobia (Fear of becoming
bald)
  </label>
  <label>
      <input type="checkbox" name="phobia"
value="Beards" checked>Pogonophobia (Fear of
beards)
  </label>
  <label>
      <input type="checkbox" name="phobia"
value="Bed">Clinophobia (Fear of going to bed)
  </label>
  <label>
      <input type="checkbox" name="phobia"
value="Chins" checked>Geniophobia (Fear of
chins)
  </label>
  <label>
      <input type="checkbox" name="phobia"
value="Flowers">Anthophobia (Fear of flowers)
  </label>
  <label>
      <input type="checkbox" name="phobia"
value="Flying">Aviatophobia (Fear of flying)
  </label>
  <label>
      <input type="checkbox" name="phobia"
value="Purple">Porphyrophobia (Fear of purple)
```

```
            </label>
        <label>
            <input type="checkbox" name="phobia"
        value="Teeth" checked>Odontophobia (Fear of
        teeth)
            </label>
        <label>
            <input type="checkbox" name="phobia"
        value="Thinking">Phronemophobia (Fear of
        thinking)
            </label>
        <label>
            <input type="checkbox" name="phobia" value
        ="Vegetables">Lachanophobia (Fear of vegetables)
            </label>
        <label>
            <input type="checkbox" name="phobia"
        value="Fear" checked>Phobophobia (Fear of fear)
            </label>
        <label>
            <input type="checkbox" name="phobia"
        value="Everything">Pantophobia (Fear of
        everything)
            </label>
    </fieldset>
```

Some notes about this code:

- » You use the `<fieldset>` tag to group a collection of related form fields together.

- » You use the `<legend>` tag to create a caption for the parent `fieldset` element. Figure 4-2 shows how this looks in the browser.

- » Because the `<input>` tags are wrapped in their respective `<label>` tags, the user can select or deselect each checkbox by clicking the checkbox itself or by clicking its label.

- » To get each checkbox on its own line, I added the declaration `display: block` to the CSS for the `label` element.

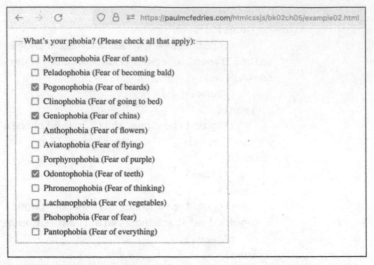

What's your phobia? (Please check all that apply):

- ☐ Myrmecophobia (Fear of ants)
- ☐ Peladophobia (Fear of becoming bald)
- ☑ Pogonophobia (Fear of beards)
- ☐ Clinophobia (Fear of going to bed)
- ☑ Geniophobia (Fear of chins)
- ☐ Anthophobia (Fear of flowers)
- ☐ Aviatophobia (Fear of flying)
- ☐ Porphyrophobia (Fear of purple)
- ☑ Odontophobia (Fear of teeth)
- ☐ Phronemophobia (Fear of thinking)
- ☐ Lachanophobia (Fear of vegetables)
- ☑ Phobophobia (Fear of fear)
- ☐ Pantophobia (Fear of everything)

FIGURE 4-2: Some checkbox form fields, wrapped in a `fieldset` group with a `legend` element.

Setting Up Radio Buttons

If you want to offer your users a collection of related options, only one of which can be selected at a time, then radio buttons (sometimes called option buttons) are the way to go. Form radio buttons congregate in groups of two or more, and only one button in the group can be selected at any time. If the user clicks another button in that group, it becomes selected and the previously selected button becomes deselected.

You create a radio button using the following variation of the `<input>` tag:

```
<input type="radio" name="radioGroup"
    value="radioValue" [checked]>
```

The various parts of this code are as follows:

>> *radioGroup:* The name you want to assign to the group of radio buttons. All the radio buttons that use the same name value belong to that group.

>> *radioValue:* The value you want to assign to the radio button. If this radio button is selected when the form is submitted, this is the value that is sent.

>> checked: When this optional attribute is present, the radio button is initially selected.

Here's an example, and Figure 4-3 shows what happens:

```
<fieldset>
    <legend>
        Select a delivery method
    </legend>
    <div>
        <input type="radio" id="carrier-pigeon"
name="delivery" value="pigeon" checked>
        <label for="carrier-pigeon">Carrier
pigeon</label>
    </div>
    <div>
        <input type="radio" id="pony-express"
name="delivery" value="pony">
        <label for="pony-express">Pony express
</label>
    </div>
    <div>
        <input type="radio" id="snail-mail"
name="delivery" value="postal">
        <label for="snail-mail">Snail mail</label>
    </div>
    <div>
        <input type="radio" id="some-punk"
name="delivery" value="bikecourier">
        <label for="some-punk">Some punk on a
bike</label>
    </div>
</fieldset>
```

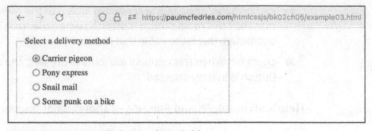

FIGURE 4-3: Some radio button form fields.

Making Selection Lists

Selection lists are common sights in HTML forms because they enable the web developer to display a relatively large number of choices in a compact control that most users know how to operate. When deciding between a checkbox, radio button group, or selection list, here are some rough guidelines to follow:

>> If an option or setting has only two values that can be represented by on and off, use a checkbox.

>> If the option or setting has three or four values, use a group of three or four radio buttons.

>> If the option or setting has five or more values, use a selection list.

This section shows you how to create selection lists. As you work through this part, it'll help to remember that a selection list is really an amalgam of two types of fields: the list container and the options within that container. The former is a `select` element and the latter is a collection of `option` elements.

To create the list container, you use the `<select>` tag:

```
<select name="selectName" size="selectSize"
    [multiple]>
```

The various parts of this code are as follows:

- ≫ *selectName*: The name you want to assign to the selection list.

- ≫ *selectSize*: The optional number of rows in the selection list box that are visible. If you omit this value, the browser displays the list as a drop-down box.

- ≫ multiple: When this optional attribute is present, the user is allowed to select multiple options in the list.

For each item in the list, you add an ‹option› tag between the ‹select› and ‹/select› tags:

```
<option value="optionValue" [selected]>
```

The various parts of this code are as follows:

- ≫ *optionValue*: The value you want to assign to the list option.

- ≫ selected: When this optional attribute is present, the list option is initially selected.

Here are some examples:

```
<form>
    <div>
        <label for="hair-color">Select your hair
    color:</label><br>
        <select id="hair-color" name="hair-color">
            <option value="black">Black</option>
            <option value="blonde">Blonde</option>
            <option value="brunette"
    selected>Brunette</option>
            <option value="red">Red</option>
            <option value="neon">Something neon
    </option>
            <option value="none">None</option>
        </select>
    </div>
    <div>
        <label for="hair-style">Select your hair
    style:</label><br>
```

```
        <select id="hair-style" name="hair-style"
size="4">
        <option value="bouffant">Bouffant
</option>
        <option value="mohawk">Mohawk</option>
        <option value="page-boy">Page Boy
</option>
        <option value="permed">Permed</option>
        <option value="shag">Shag</option>
        <option value="straight"
selected>Straight</option>
        <option value="none">Style? What
style?</option>
      </select>
  </div>
  <div>
      <label for="hair-products">Hair products
used in the last year:</label><br>
      <select id="hair-products" name="hair-
products" size="5" multiple>
        <option value="gel">Gel</option>
        <option value="grecian-
formula">Grecian Formula</option>
        <option value="mousse">Mousse</option>
        <option value="peroxide">Peroxide
</option>
        <option value="shoe-black">Shoe
black</option>
      </select>
    </div>
  </form>
```

There are three lists here (refer to Figure 4-4):

>> hair-color: This list doesn't specify a size, so the browser
   displays it as a drop-down list.
>> hair-style: This list uses a size value of 4, so four options
   are visible in the list.
>> hair-products: This list uses a size value of 5, so five
   options are visible in the list. Also, the multiple attribute is
   set, so you can select multiple options in the list.

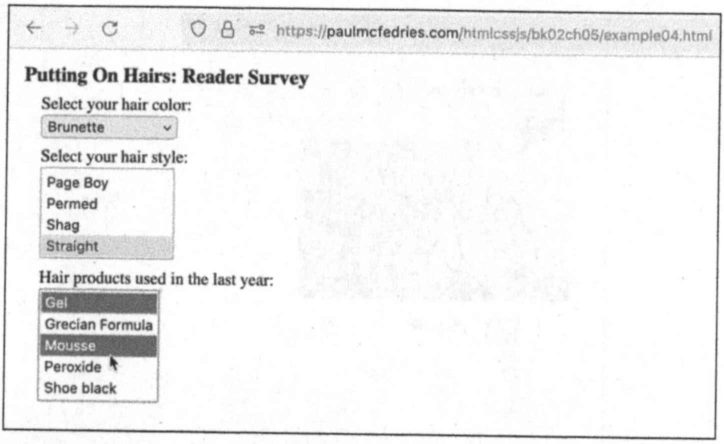

FIGURE 4-4: Some examples of selection lists.

Adding a Picker or Two

HTML also offers a number of other <input> tag types that fall under a category I call "pickers," meaning that in each case the field displays a button that, when clicked, opens a control that enables the user to pick a value. Here's a quick look at the available pickers:

>> color: Opens a color picker dialog that enables the user to choose a color. The color picker varies depending on the browser and operating system; Figure 4-5 shows the Google Chrome for the Mac version. Set the value attribute in the #rrggbb format to specify an initial color (the default is black: #000000). Here's an example:

```
<input type="color" name="bg-color" value=
    "#4f5392">
```

If the text #rrggbb is meaningless to you, not to worry: I explain it in satisfying detail in Chapter 8.

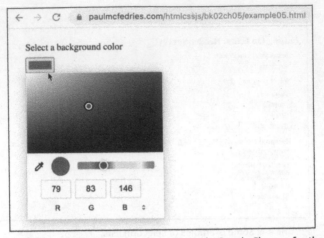

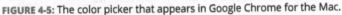

FIGURE 4-5: The color picker that appears in Google Chrome for the Mac.

>> date: Opens a date picker dialog so that the user can choose a date. Figure 4-6 shows the Microsoft Edge version. Set the value attribute in the yyyy-mm-dd format to specify an initial date. Note that the date the user sees may use a different format (such as mm/dd/yyyy, as shown in Figure 4-6), but the value returned by the element is always in the yyyy-mm-dd format. Here's an example:

```
<input type="date" name="appt-date" value=
    "2023-08-23">
```

>> file: Displays a Choose File button (refer to Figure 4-7) that, when clicked, opens the user's operating system's file picker dialog so that the user can select a file. You can add the multiple attribute to enable the user to select more than one file. Here's an example:

```
<input type="file" name="user-photo">
```

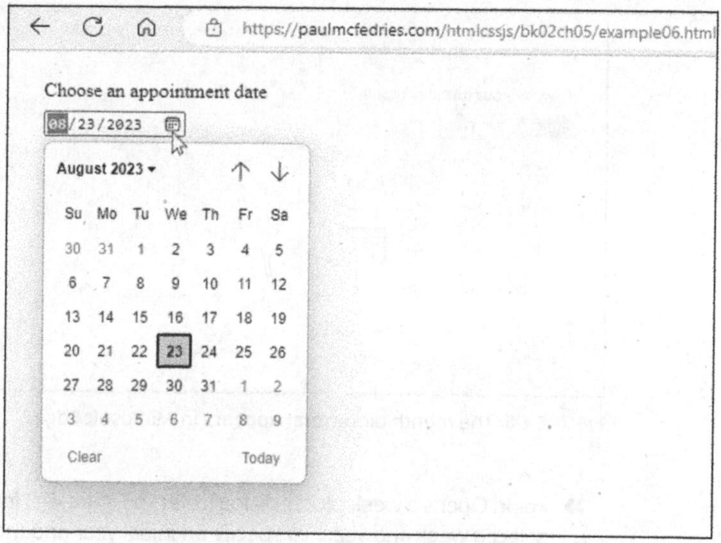

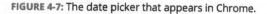

Choose an appointment date

08 / 23 / 2023 📅

August 2023 ▾				↑	↓	
Su	Mo	Tu	We	Th	Fr	Sa
30	31	1	2	3	4	5
6	7	8	9	10	11	12
13	14	15	16	17	18	19
20	21	22	23	24	25	26
27	28	29	30	31	1	2
3	4	5	6	7	8	9
Clear					Today	

FIGURE 4-6: The date picker that appears in Microsoft Edge.

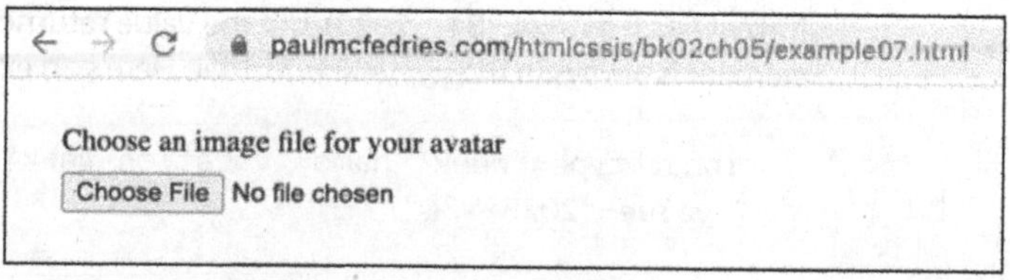

Choose an image file for your avatar

Choose File | No file chosen

FIGURE 4-7: The date picker that appears in Chrome.

» month: Opens a month picker dialog (refer to Figure 4-8) to enable the user to choose a month and year. Set the value attribute in the yyyy–mm format to specify an initial month and year. The value the user sees may be in a different format (such as August 2023), but the value returned by the element is always in the yyyy–mm format. Here's an example:

```
<input type="month" name="birthday-month"
    value="2023-08">
```

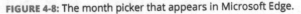

FIGURE 4-8: The month picker that appears in Microsoft Edge.

>> **week:** Opens a week picker dialog (refer to Figure 4-9) for the user to select a week and year. To specify an initial year and month, set the `value` attribute in the yyyy–W*nn* format, where *nn* is the two-digit week number. The value shown to the user may be in another format (such as Week 34, 2023), but the value returned by the element is always in the yyyy–W*nn* format. Here's an example:

```
<input type="week" name="vacation-week"
    value="2023-W34">
```

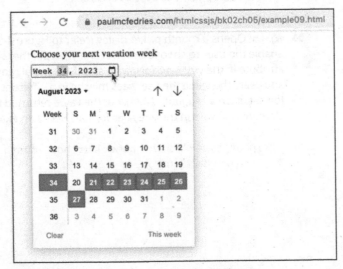

FIGURE 4-9: The week picker that appears in Chrome.

IN THIS CHAPTER

» Wrapping your head around the CSS box model

» Giving elements room to breathe with padding

» Enclosing elements with borders

» Keeping other elements at bay with margins

» Setting the width and height of page elements

Chapter **5**

Exploring the CSS Box Model

C SS comes with a huge number of tools and techniques that you can wield to make stubborn page elements behave themselves. Those tools and techniques form the bulk of this book, but just about everything you do as a CSS developer will in some way involve (or be influenced by) the CSS box model, which is the subject you delve into in this chapter. The box model is so fundamental to almost everything in CSS that you should consider this chapter to be the foundation for almost every other CSS topic in the book.

Getting to Know the Box Model

Every web page consists of a series of HTML tags, and each of those tags represents an element on the page. In the strange and geeky world known as Style Sheet Land, each of these elements is considered to have an invisible box around it (okay, it's a very strange world). That may not sound like a big deal, but those boxes are the royal road to CSS mastery.

Touring the box model

Figure 5-1 shows what the aforementioned invisible box looks like in the abstract, and Figure 5-2 shows an actual page element.

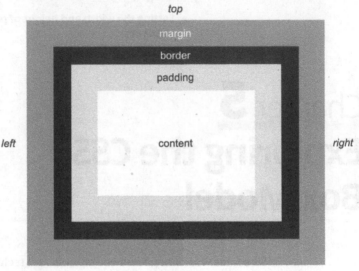

FIGURE 5-1: The components of the CSS box model.

Figures 5-1 and 5-2 show the following box components:

>> **Content:** The stuff inside the box, such as text, links, lists, images, and video. In other words, the content of all the boxes in your page is nothing more nor less than the actual content you've added to the page. The four sides of the content area — that is, its top, left, bottom, and right edges — define the *content box*.

>> **Padding:** The space that surrounds the content. That is, it's the space just outside the content, but inside the border (discussed next). Refer to "Putting on Some Padding," later in this chapter, to find out more about messing around with the padding. The four sides of the padding area define the *padding box*.

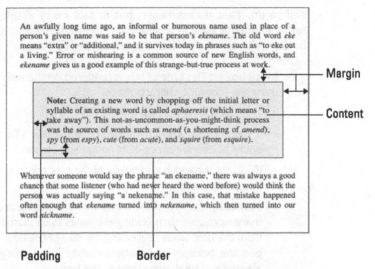

An awfully long time ago, an informal or humorous name used in place of a person's given name was said to be that person's *ekename*. The old word *eke* means "extra" or "additional," and it survives today in phrases such as "to eke out a living." Error or mishearing is a common source of new English words, and *ekename* gives us a good example of this strange-but-true process at work.

Note: Creating a new word by chopping off the initial letter or syllable of an existing word is called *aphaeresis* (which means "to take away"). This not-as-uncommon-as-you-might-think process was the source of words such as *mend* (a shortening of *amend*), *spy* (from *espy*), *cute* (from *acute*), and *squire* (from *esquire*).

Whenever someone would say the phrase "an ekename," there was always a good chance that some listener (who had never heard the word before) would think the person was actually saying "a nekename." In this case, that mistake happened often enough that *ekename* turned into *nekename*, which then turned into our word *nickname*.

— Margin

— Content

Padding   Border

FIGURE 5-2: The CSS box model applied to an actual page element.

>> **Border:** The space that surrounds the padding. That is, it's the space just outside the padding, but inside the margin (discussed next). Refer to "Building a Border," later in this chapter, to get a good look at how you can manipulate borders with CSS. The four sides of the border define the *border box.*

>> **Margin:** The space that surrounds the border. That is, it's the space just outside the border. The four sides of the margin define the *margin box.*

Note that the padding, border, and margin are all "optional" in the sense that you can use CSS rules to shrink them down to nothing. Also, the top, left, bottom, and right edges of the padding box, border box, and margin box all have corresponding CSS properties that you can play around with.

Getting the hand of block and inline boxes

You may be tempted to think that these invisible boxes only surround block-level elements, which are those elements that start new sections of text: p, blockquote, h1 through h6, div, all the page layout semantic tags, such as header, article, and section, and so on. That makes sense, but in fact every single tag, even inline elements such as a and span, have a box around them. So, in the end, you always deal with two types of boxes:

>> **Block boxes:** This type of box is rendered on the web page using the following characteristics:

- The box starts on a new line.
- If you don't set a width for the box, the box will fill the entire horizontal space of its containing element.
- If you set the width and height of the box, those properties get applied.
- Increasing the size of the box padding, borders, and margins causes surrounding elements to be pushed away from the box, while decreasing the size of the box padding, borders, and margins causes surrounding elements to be drawn closer to the box.

By definition, the default value for the display property of a block box is block:

```
display: block;
```

>> **Inline boxes:** This type of box is rendered on the web page as follows:

- The box flows along with the surrounding content.
- The box will only be as wide as its content requires.
- If you set the width and height of the box, those properties do not get applied.
- Increasing or decreasing the size of the vertical padding, borders, and margins has no effect on the surrounding elements.
- Increasing the size of the horizontal padding, borders, and margins causes surrounding elements to be pushed away from the box, while decreasing the size of the horizontal padding, borders, and margins causes surrounding elements to be drawn closer to the box.

By definition, the default value for the display property of an inline box is inline:

```
display: inline;
```

Putting on Some Padding

In the CSS box model, the *padding* is the space that surrounds the content out to the border.

There are four sections to the padding — above, to the right of, below, and to the left of the content — so CSS offers four corresponding properties for adding padding to an element:

```
selector {
    padding-top: top-value;
    padding-right: right-value;
    padding-bottom: bottom-value;
    padding-left: left-value;
}
```

The various parts of this code are as follows:

- **>>** *selector*: A CSS selector that specifies the item (or items) you want to style.

- **>>** *top-value* (and so on): A number followed by a CSS measurement unit (such as px, em, rem, vw, or vh; refer to Chapter 7 to find out what these units mean) or a percentage.

Figure 5-3 shows a chunk of text with a border, but no padding. The result is that the content is uncomfortably close to the border, making the text feel cramped.

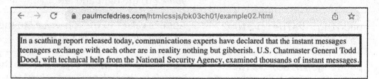

FIGURE 5-3: Some text with a border, but no padding.

Figure 5-4 shows how much nicer the text looks when I apply the following rule to the text (which is inside a `<p>` tag):

```css
p {
    padding-top: 16px;
    padding-right: 12px;
    padding-bottom: 16px;
    padding-left: 20px;
}
```

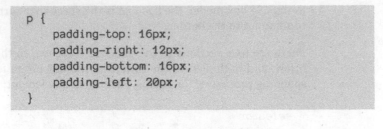

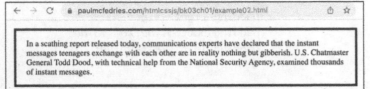

In a scathing report released today, communications experts have declared that the instant messages teenagers exchange with each other are in reality nothing but gibberish. U.S. Chatmaster General Todd Dood, with technical help from the National Security Agency, examined thousands of instant messages.

FIGURE 5-4: The same text from Figure 5-3, with padding added.

CSS also offers a shorthand syntax that uses the `padding` property. There are four different syntaxes you can use with the `padding` property, and they're all listed in Table 5-1.

TABLE 5-1 ## The padding Shorthand Property

Syntax	Description
padding: *value1*;	Applies *value1* to all four sides
padding: *value1* *value2*;	Applies *value1* to the top and bottom and *value2* to the right and left
padding: *value1* *value2* *value3*;	Applies *value1* to the top, *value2* to the right and left, and *value3* to the bottom
padding: *value1* *value2* *value3* *value4*;	Applies value1 to the top, value2 to the right, value3 to the bottom, and value4 to the left

Here's how you'd rewrite the previous example using the `padding` shorthand:

```css
p {
    padding: 16px 12px 16px 20px;
}
```

Building a Border

Modern web design eschews vertical and horizontal lines as a means of separating content, preferring instead to let copious amounts of whitespace do the job. However, that doesn't mean you should never use lines in your designs, particularly borders. An element's *border* is the notional set of lines that enclose the element's content and padding. Borders are an often useful way to make it clear that an element is separate from the surrounding elements in the page.

Applying a border

There are four lines associated with an element's border — above, to the right of, below, and to the left of the padding — so CSS offers four properties for adding borders to an element:

```
selector {
    border-top: top-width top-style top-color;
    border-right: right-width right-style
    right-color;
    border-bottom: bottom-width bottom-style
    bottom-color;
    border-left: left-width left-style left-color;
}
```

Each border requires three values:

>> **Width:** The thickness of the border line, which you specify using a number followed by a CSS measurement unit (such as px, em, rem, vw, or vh). Note, however, that most border widths are measured in pixels, usually 1px. You can also specify one of the following keywords: thin, medium, or thick (although note that the thickness associated with each keyword isn't defined in the CSS standard, so your mileage may vary depending on the browser).

>> **Style:** The type of border line, which must be one of the following keywords:

● dotted: Displays the border as a series of dots.

● dashed: Displays the border as a series of dashes.

● solid: Displays the border as an uninterrupted line.

- `double`: Displays the border as two solid, parallel lines.
- `groove`: Displays the border as though it's carved into the page as a v-shaped trough (the opposite effect of `ridge`).
- `ridge` Displays the border as though it's raised from the page as a v-shaped extrusion (the opposite effect of `groove`).
- `inset`: Displays the border as though it was embedded into the page (the opposite effect of `outset`).
- `outset`: Displays the border as though it was embossed on the page (the opposite effect of `inset`).

Figure 5-5 shows an example of each style. (I used 24px as the border width for the groove, ridge, inset, and outset styles because their effects are hard to discern at smaller widths.)

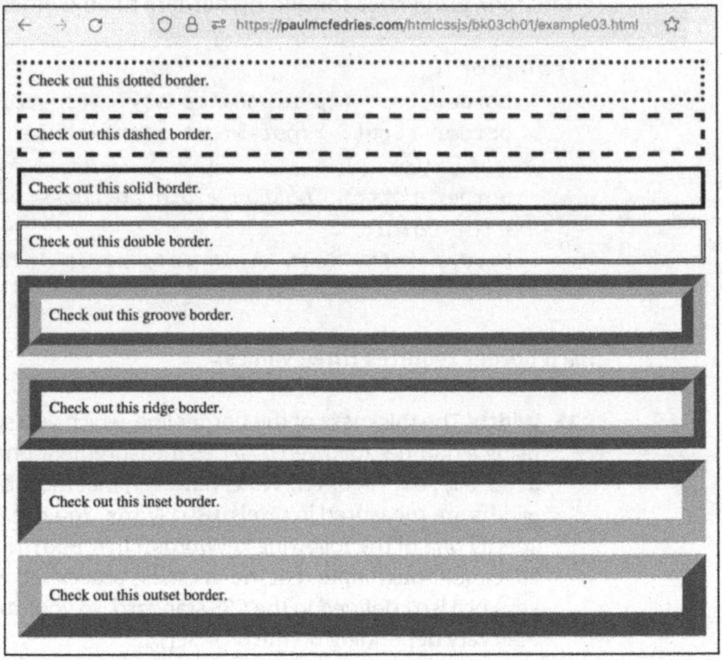

FIGURE 5-5: The border style keywords in action.

>> **Color:** The color of the border line. You can use a color keyword, an `rgb()` function, an `hsl()` function, or an RGB code, as I describe in Chapter 8.

Here's an example that adds a 1-pixel, dashed, red bottom border to the header element:

```
header {
    border-bottom: 1px dashed red;
}
```

At times in your CSS work, you may need to focus on a very specific part of the border. For example, you may want to work with just the style of the bottom border or the color of the left border. No problem!

You can use any of the following properties, for example, to work with a specific border width (where *border-width* is a width in any CSS measurement unit):

```
border-top-width: border-width;
border-right-width: border-width;
border-bottom-width: border-width;
border-left-width: border-width;
```

Similarly, you can use any of the following properties to work with a specific border style (where *border-style* is any valid border style keyword, such as solid or dashed):

```
border-top-style: border-style;
border-right-style: border-style;
border-bottom-style: border-style;
border-left-style: border-style;
```

And finally, you can use any of the following properties to work with a specific border color (where *border-color* is any valid CSS color):

```
border-top-color: border-color;
border-right-color: border-color;
border-bottom-color: border-color;
border-left-color: border-color;
```

If you want to add a full border around an element and you want all four sides to use the same width, style, and color, you'll be glad to know that CSS mercifully offers a shorthand version that uses the border property:

```
border: width style color;
```

Here's an example:

```
border: 4px solid black;
```

TIP

Technically, the only value that's required by the border shorthand property is *style*. If you declare something like border: solid, the browser draws a solid border with a 3px width and a dark-gray color.

Rounding a border

The boxes in the box model are resolutely rectangular, but that doesn't mean you have to always settle for sharp corners when you add a border around an element. To give your borders a softer look, you can round them using the border-radius property, which can round one or more corners based on the arc of either a circle or an ellipse.

The most common and most straightforward way to round an element's border corners is to base the rounding on the arc of a circle with a specified radius. Here's the border-radius syntax to use for this case:

```
selector {
    border-radius: radius;
}
```

The various parts of this code are as follows:

» *selector*: A CSS selector that specifies the item (or items) you want to style.

» *radius*: A value (expressed on one of the standard CSS measurement units, such as px, em, rem, vw, or vh) or a percentage.

The radius you're specifying here is the radius of a circle. Figure 5-6 shows how this works. The element on the left has no border radius, so it's got the default right-angled corners. The element on the right has a border radius of 100px set on the top-right corner. (I show you how to specify individual corners shortly.) Notice how the rounded corner of the border follows an arc of the inscribed circle. That circle has a radius of 100px. The bigger the radius value, the bigger the circle, so the more rounded the corner.

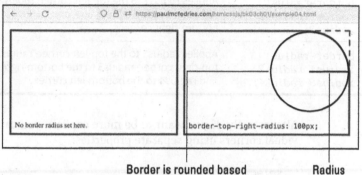

Border is rounded based   Radius
on an arc of a circle

FIGURE 5-6: How CSS rounds a border based on the arc of a circle.

For example, suppose you have an aside element that has a border you want to round slightly. Here's some CSS that'll do it:

```
aside {
    border: 1px solid black;
    border-radius: 10px;
}
```

The preceding border-radius syntax is a shorthand version that applies a single radius value to all four corners. There are actually four different syntaxes you can use with the border-radius property, and they're all listed in Table 5-2.

TABLE 5-2 The Extended border-radius Shorthand Property

Syntax	Description
border-radius: radius1;	Applies *radius1* to all four corners
border-radius: radius1 radius2;	Applies *radius1* to the top-left and bottom-right corners and *radius2* to the top-right and bottom-left corners
border-radius: radius1 radius2 radius3;	Applies *radius1* to the top-left corner, *radius2* to the top-right and bottom-left corners, and *radius3* to the bottom-right corner
border-radius: radius1 radius2 radius3 radius4;	Applies radius1 to the top-left corner, radius2 to the top-right corner, radius3 to the bottom-right corner, and radius4 to the bottom-left corner

Alternatively, if you want to be more explicit, you can style individual corners using separate properties:

```
selector {
    border-top-left-radius: radiusTL;
    border-top-right-radius: radiusTR;
    border-bottom-right-radius: radiusBR;
    border-bottom-left-radius: radiusBL;
}
```

For example, the following two CSS rules do the same rounding job:

```
aside {
    border: 1px solid black;
    border-radius: 50px 100px 10px;
}
```

```
aside {
    border: 1px solid black;
    border-top-left-radius: 50px;
    border-top-right-radius: 100px;
    border-bottom-right-radius: 10px;
    border-bottom-left-radius: 100px;
}
```

Messing with Margins

The final component of the CSS box model is the *margin*, which is the space around the border of the box. Margins are an important detail in web design because they prevent elements from rubbing up against the edges of the browser content area, ensure that two elements don't overlap each other (unless you want them to), and create a pleasing amount of whitespace between elements.

As with padding, there are four sections to the margin — above, to the right of, below, and to the left of the border — so CSS offers four corresponding properties for adding margins to an element:

```
selector {
    margin-top: top-value;
    margin-right: right-value;
    margin-bottom: bottom-value;
    margin-left: left-value;
}
```

The various parts of this code are as follows:

» *selector*: A CSS selector that specifies the item (or items) you want to style

» *top-value*, etc.: A number followed by a CSS measurement unit (such as px, em, rem, vw, or vh; refer to Chapter 7 to find out what these units mean) or a percentage

Here's an example:

```
aside {
    margin-top: 16px;
    margin-right: 8px;
    margin-bottom: 32px;
    margin-left: 24px;
}
```

TIP

If you want to center a block element horizontally within its parent, you can do it with margins. First, you need to give the element a width (refer to "Styling Sizes," later in this chapter). Then add the following to a rule that targets the element:

```
margin-right: auto;
margin-left: auto;
```

As it does for padding, CSS also offers a shorthand syntax for the margin property. Table 5-3 lists the four syntaxes you can use with the margin property.

TABLE 5-3 **The margin Shorthand Property**

Syntax	Description
margin: *value1*;	Applies *value1* to all four sides
margin: *value1* *value2*;	Applies *value1* to the top and bottom and *value2* to the right and left
margin: *value1* *value2* *value3*;	Applies *value1* to the top, *value2* to the right and left, and *value3* to the bottom
margin: *value1* *value2* *value3* *value4*;	Applies value1 to the top, value2 to the right, value3 to the bottom, and value4 to the left

Here's the shorthand version of the previous example:

```
aside {
    margin: 16px 8px 32px 24px;
}
```

Styling Sizes

When the web browser renders a page, it examines each element and sets the dimensions of that element. For block-level elements such as <header> and <div>, the browser sets the dimensions as follows:

» **Width:** Set to the width of the element's containing block. Because by default the width of the <body> element is set to the width of the browser's content area, in practice all block-level elements have their widths set to the width of the content area.

» **Height:** Set just high enough to hold all the element's content.

You alter an element's dimensions by styling its width and height properties:

```
selector {
    width: width-value;
    height: height-value;
}
```

The various parts of this code are as follows:

» *selector*: A CSS selector that specifies the item (or items) you want to style.

» *width-value, height-value*: One of the following:

- *A number:* Be sure to follow the number with one of the CSS measurement units I talk about in Chapter 7 (such as px, em, rem, vw, or vh).

- *A percentage:* The resulting value is the percentage applied to the corresponding dimension of the element's containing block. If you're setting the width, the value is the percentage times the containing element's width; if you're setting the height, the value is the percentage times the containing element's height.

- *A keyword:* For the width property, you have three choices here:

  fit-content: Sets the width big enough to include all the element's text. If there's more text than can fit into the width of the containing element, the text is wrapped within that container.

  max-content: Sets the width big enough to include all the element's text. If there's more text than can fit into the width of the containing element, the text is *not* wrapped.

Note that a long text entry may therefore extend beyond its containing element.

`min-content`: Sets the width to the width of the longest word in the element's text. All the element's text wraps within this width.

For example, if you have an `aside` element that you want to take up only three quarters of the width of its containing element, you use the following rule:

```
aside {
    width: 75%;
}
```

Figure 5-7 shows a page that consists of a main div element that acts as the container for several `p` elements, each of which tries out a different `width` value.

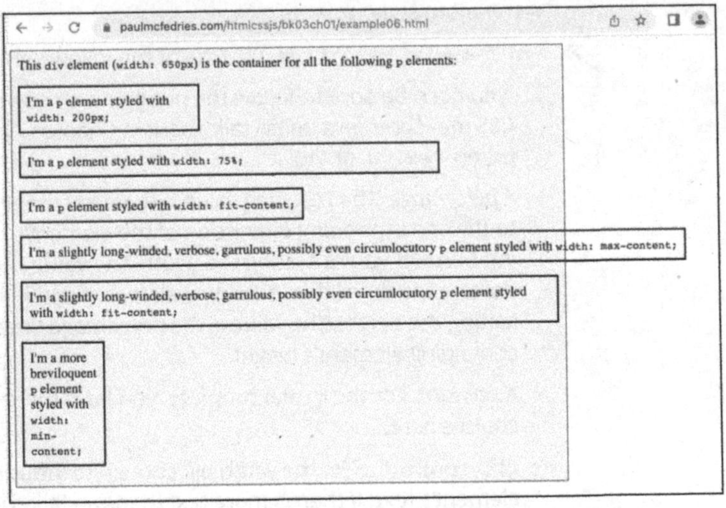

paulmcfedries.com/htmlcssjs/bk03ch01/example06.html
This div element (width: 650px) is the container for all the following p elements:
I'm a p element styled with width: 200px;
I'm a p element styled with width: 75%;
I'm a p element styled with width: fit-content;
I'm a slightly long-winded, verbose, garrulous, possibly even circumlocutory p element styled with width: max-content;
I'm a slightly long-winded, verbose, garrulous, possibly even circumlocutory p element styled with width: fit-content;
I'm a more breviloquent p element styled with width: min-content;

FIGURE 5-7: Putting different values of the `width` property to work.

REMEMBER

Most of the time you'll mess only with an element's width; getting the height right is notoriously difficult because it depends on too many factors: the content, the browser's window size, the user's default font size, and more.

Specifying a minimum or maximum height or width

Sometimes (quite often, actually), to make a page design work, you need an element to always be rendered at least at some specified height or width, even if the element's content would normally dictate smaller dimensions. If the element ends up with more content than can fit in the specified height or width, it's okay for the element to expand as needed.

What I'm talking about here is setting a minimum height or width on an element, which you can do just like that by working with the min-height and min-width properties:

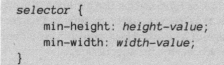

```
selector {
    min-height: height-value;
    min-width: width-value;
}
```

The various parts of this code are as follows:

» *selector*: A CSS selector that specifies the item (or items) you want to style.

» *width-value, height-value*: Use a number (followed by a unit such as px, em, rem, vw, or vh; check out Chapter 7), a percentage, or a keyword (max-content, min-content, or auto, which lets the browser decide).

For example, if a section element must be at least 200 pixels high no matter what content it contains, use the following rule:

```
section {
    min-height: 200px;
}
```

The opposite concern is when you don't want an element's height or width to grow beyond a particular value. The element's height or width can be less than that value, but never more than that value, even if it has more content than can fit.

To accomplish this goal, you need to set a maximum height or width on an element, which you can do by working with the max-height and max-width properties:

```
selector {
    max-height: height-value;
    max-width: width-value;
}
```

The various parts of this code are as follows:

>> *selector*: A CSS selector that specifies the item (or items) you want to style.

>> *width-value*, *height-value*: Use a number (followed by a unit such as px, em, rem, vw, or vh; refer to Chapter 7), a percentage, or a keyword (max-content, min-content, or auto, which lets the browser decide).

For example, if an aside element must be no more than 200 pixels high and no more than 150 pixels wide, no matter what content it contains, use the following rule:

```
footer {
    max-height: 200px;
    max-width: 150px;
}
```

Making width and height easier

When you're working with an element's dimensions, you have to take into account its padding widths and border sizes if you want to get things right. Believe me, taking all that into account is no picnic. Fortunately, help is just around the corner. You can avoid all those extra calculations by forcing the web browser to be sensible and define an element's size to include not just the content, but the padding and border as well. A CSS property called box-sizing is the superhero here:

```
selector {
    box-sizing: border-box;
}
```

The declaration `box-sizing: border-box` tells the browser to set the element's height and width to include the content, padding, and border. You could add this declaration to all your block-level element rules, but that's way too much work. Instead, you can use a trick in which you use an asterisk (*) selector, which is a short-hand way of referencing every element on the page:

```
* {
    box-sizing: border-box;
}
```

Put this at the top of your style sheet, and then you never have to worry about it again.

IN THIS CHAPTER

» Figuring out parents, children, siblings, and other CSS kinfolk

» Understanding why selectors are so darned important

» Selecting elements by type, class, or id

» Targeting child and sibling elements

» Getting a handle on pseudo-classes

Chapter **6**

Selecting Stuff with Selectors

I n this chapter, you investigate the rich, useful, and incredibly powerful realm of CSS selectors. I take you through not only all the must-know selectors that are part of the coding repertoire of every web designer, but also a satisfyingly extensive tour of the broader selector toolkit.

Understanding Element Relationships

One of the key concepts in this chapter — and, indeed, one of the most useful concepts in all of CSS — is the set of relationships that exist between every element in a web page.

To help you understand these relationships, it's useful to have an example to refer to over the next page or two, so here you go:

```
<html lang="en">
    <head>
        <meta charset="UTF-8">
```

```
        <title>So Many Kale Recipes</title>
    </head>
    <body>
        <header>
            <h1>Above and Beyond the Kale of
Duty</h1>
        </header>
        <main>
            <p>
                Do you love to cook with kale?
            </p>
            <p>
                Do you know the history of kale?
            </p>
            <p>
                Are you obsessed with kale?
            </p>
        </main>
    </body>
</html>
```

As shown in Figure 6-1, one way to look at this code is as a set of nested containers:

>> The html element includes every other element in the page, so its container surrounds everything.

>> Within the html element are two smaller containers: the head and body elements.

>> Within the head element are containers for the meta and title elements.

>> Within the body element are containers for the header and main elements.

>> Within the header element is a container for the h1 element.

>> Within the main element are containers for three p elements.

```
<html>
  <head>
    <meta>
                          <title>
                             So Many Kale Recipes

    <body>
      <header>                    <main>
        <h1>                         <p>              <p>              <p>
           Above and Beyond the        Do you love to     Do you know the    Are you obsessed
           Kale of Duty                cook with kale?    history of kale?   with kale?
```

FIGURE 6-1: The web page code as a set of nested containers.

The key point here is the nesting of these containers because it's the nesting that determines the relationships that each element has to every other element. Here's how it works:

>> If element P contains element C, then element P is said to be the *parent* of element C. In Figure 6-1, for example, the body element is the parent of the header and main elements.

>> If element C is contained in element P, then element C is said to be the *child* of element P. In Figure 6-1, for example, the h1 element is the child of the header element.

>> If both element C1 and C2 are contained in element P, then C1 and C2 are said to be *siblings* of each other. In Figure 6-1, for example, the three p elements in the main element are siblings.

>> If element C is contained in element P, and element D is contained in element C, then element D is said to be a *descendant* of element P, and element P is an *ancestor* of element D. In Figure 6-1, for example, the h1 element is a descendant of the body element. Similarly, the body element is an ancestor of any of the p elements.

I threw a lot of new terminology at you in that list, so don't worry if it hasn't all sunk in just yet. These concepts will quickly become second nature to you as you work with CSS in general and selectors in particular.

Getting to Know the Selector

Okay, so just what is a selector, anyway? A *selector* is a pattern that you use to define, as accurately as possible, which element or elements on the page you want to style.

A generic CSS rule looks like this:

```
selector {
    one or more CSS declarations go here
}
```

What this rule says, in effect is, "Excuse me! Given whatever element or elements are matched by `selector`, please apply all the styles that are given in the declaration block that follows. Thanks so much."

Any element referenced by a selector is known as the *subject* of the selector.

One of the most powerful aspects of selectors is that you can take a single CSS declaration block and apply it to multiple selectors. For example, you may need to apply exactly the same styling to your page's nav and footer elements.

Applying the same styling to multiple elements isn't a problem because you can create a *selector list* that enables you to add as many selectors as you need instead of creating separate (and identical) CSS rules for each element. In your list, each selector is separated by a comma:

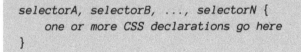

```
selectorA, selectorB, ..., selectorN {
    one or more CSS declarations go here
}
```

For easier reading, most web developers put each selector on its own line, like so:

```
selectorA,
selectorB,
...,
```

```
selectorN {
    one or more CSS declarations go here
}
```

Okay, enough theory. It's time to start actually selecting stuff.

Exploring the Standard Selectors

The happy news about CSS selectors is that, although there are dozens in the CSS standard, there are just a few workhorses that you'll use for most of your CSS rules. In particular, the selectors I cover in the next few sections probably deserve to be tattooed somewhere on your person for easy reference.

The type selector

The *type selector* matches page items by element name (so it's also sometimes called the *element selector* or the *tag selector*):

```
element {
    property1: value1;
    property2: value2;
    ...
}
```

For example, if you want to put a border around every aside element, you use a CSS rule like this:

```
aside {
    border: 3px solid black;
}
```

The class selector (.)

If you master just one CSS selector, make it the class selector, because you'll use it time and again in your web projects. A *class selector* is one that targets its styles at a particular web page class. So, what's a class? I'm glad you asked. A *class* is an attribute assigned to one or more tags that enables you to create a kind of grouping for those tags. Here's the syntax for adding a class to an element:

```
<element class="class-name">
```

The various parts of this code are as follows:

- » *element*: The name of the element you're working with.

- » *class-name*: The name you want to assign to the class. The name must begin with a letter, and the rest can be any combination of letters, numbers, hyphens (–), and underscores (_).

Here's an example:

```
<h2 class="subtitle">
```

With your classes assigned to your tags as needed, you're ready to start selecting those classes using CSS. You select a class by preceding the class name with a dot (.) in your style rule:

```
.class-name {
    property1: value1;
    property2: value2;
    ...
}
```

For example, here's a rule for the subtitle class:

```
.subtitle {
    color: royalblue;
    font-style: italic;
}
```

The advantage here is that you can assign the subtitle class to any tag on the page, and CSS will apply the same style rule to each of those elements.

When you use a selector such as .subtitle in a CSS rule, you're asking the browser to match every page element that uses the subtitle class. However, suppose your page uses that class not only in all its h2 elements, but all its h3 elements as well. How can you target just those h3 elements that use the subtitle class? By preceding the class selector with the element name:

```
element.class-name {
    property1: value1;
    property2: value2;
    ...
}
```

For example, the following rule matches just the h3 elements that have the subtitle class:

```
h3.subtitle {
    border: 2px dashed royalblue;
}
```

The id selector (#)

In Chapter 3, I talk about creating an anchor by adding a unique id attribute to a tag, which enables you to create a link that targeted the anchor:

```
<element id="id-name">
```

Here's an example:

```
<h1 id="page-title">
```

You can also use the id attribute as a CSS selector, which enables you to target a particular element with extreme precision. You set up this *id selector* by preceding the id value with a hashtag symbol (#) in your CSS rule:

```
#id-name {
    property1: value1;
    property2: value2;
    ...
}
```

For example, here's a rule for the page-title id:

```
#page-title {
    color: maroon;
    font-family: "Times New Roman", serif;
    text-transform: uppercase;
}
```

This isn't as useful as the tag or class selectors because it can target only a single element, which is why web developers use id selectors only rarely.

Selecting Descendants, Children, and Siblings

One of the most powerful and useful categories of CSS selectors is the collection of so-called *combinators*. These are operators (such as > and ~) that enable you to combine other types of selectors in a way that matches a specific type of relationship between the selectors: descendant, child, or sibling.

REMEMBER

The awesome power of the combinators comes from the fact that you can use them with any of the other types of selectors that you learn about in this chapter. This flexibility enables you to create truly useful CSS rules that target just the elements you want to style.

The descendant combinator ( )

To apply styles to all of an ancestor element's descendants, CSS offers the *descendant combinator*. To set up a selector that uses a descendant combinator, you include in your rule the ancestor and the descendant type you want to style, separated by a space:

```
ancestor descendant {
    property1: value1;
    property2: value2;
    ...
}
```

For example, consider the following HTML:

```
<aside>
    <h4>Links:</h4>
    <div>
        <a href="example01.html">The type
    selector</a><br>
```

```
        <a href="example02.html">The class
    selector</a><br>
        <a href="example03.html">The id selector</a>
    </div>
</aside>
```

Here's a rule that applies a few styles to the <a> tags that are descendants of the <aside> tag:

```
aside a {
    color: red;
    font-style: italic;
    text-decoration: none;
}
```

The child combinator (>)

To aim some styles at the child elements of a parent, you use the *child combinator*, where you separate the parent and child elements with a greater-than sign (>):

```
parent > child {
    property1: value1;
    property2: value2;
    ...
}
```

For example, here's a rule that targets any h4 element that's a child of an aside element:

```
aside > h4 {
    color: green;
    border-top: 3px solid black;
    border-bottom: 5px double black;
    padding: 4px 0;
    text-transform: uppercase;
}
```

The subsequent-sibling combinator (~)

One common CSS task is to apply a style rule to a particular subject that meets the following criteria:

» The target element appears in the HTML after a specified element, which is known as the *reference* element.

» The target element and the reference element are siblings.

To apply some styles to such a subject, you use the *subsequent-sibling combinator*, where you separate the reference and target elements with a tilde (~):

```
reference ~ target {
    property1: value1;
    property2: value2;
    . . .
}
```

For example, here's a rule that targets any ul element that's a subsequent sibling of an h2 element:

```
h2 ~ ul {
    background: lightpink;
    border: 5px outset crimson;
    list-style-type: square;
    padding: 8px 20px;
}
```

The next-sibling combinator (+)

To apply a style rule to just the next sibling that comes after some reference element, you use the *next-sibling combinator*, where you separate the reference and target elements with a plus sign (+):

```
reference + target {
    property1: value1;
    property2: value2;
    . . .
}
```

For example, here's a rule that targets any p element that's the next sibling of an h2 element:

```
h2 + p {
    font-style: italic;
}
```

Working with Pseudo-Classes

A *pseudo-class* is a CSS selector that acts like a class by generically targeting elements that meet some condition.

Styling elements with pseudo-classes

All pseudo-classes begin with a colon (:), followed by one or more dash-separated words. You can use a pseudo-class on its own or modified by an element. Here's the general on-its-own syntax:

```
:pseudo-class {
    property1: value1;
    property2: value2;
    ...
}
```

Using a pseudo-class on its own means your rule matches every element that meets the pseudo-class's underlying condition.

To style every element that's a first child of its parent element, you use the :first-child pseudo-class:

```
:first-child {
    font-style: italic;
}
```

However, you're more likely to want to apply your rule to first children of a specific element type. You do that by appending the element name before the pseudo-class, like so:

```
element:pseudo-class {
    property1: value1;
    property2: value2;
    ...
}
```

For example, the following rule applies a style to every p element that's a first child of its parent:

```
p:first-child {
    font-style: italic;
}
```

You can combine pseudo-classes with other selectors, particularly the combinators. For example, the following rule applies a style to every p element that's a first child of an article element:

```
article > p:first-child {
    font-style: italic;
}
```

Another common way to combine pseudo-classes and selectors is to modify the element name with a class, like so:

```
element.class:pseudo-class {
    property1: value1;
    property2: value2;
    ...
}
```

For example, the following rule applies a style to every p element that uses the intro class and is a first child of its parent:

```
p.intro:first-child {
    font-style: italic;
}
```

CSS offers several dozen pseudo-classes. Yep, several *dozen*. If that sounds like an alarming amount, don't worry: Many — perhaps even the majority of — pseudo-classes are on the obscure side and are used only occasionally at best, even by professionals. In the next section, I give you a taste of what pseudo-classes can do by exploring some pseudo-classes that enable you to match child elements.

Matching child elements

The pseudo-classes you'll turn to most often in your CSS code are those that match child elements that meet some condition. How is this different from the child combinator (>) that I talk about earlier in this chapter? The child combinator targets *every* element that's a child of the specified parent element. What the child-related pseudo-elements do is give you a way to target specific child elements by position, such as the first, third, or last child.

:first-child

The :first-child pseudo-class targets any child element that is the first of a parent element's children:

```
element:first-child {
    property1: value1;
    property2: value2;
    ...
}
```

Note: element is the name of the element type you want to target, and it's optional. If you omit element, your rule will target everything on the page that's a first child.

For example, in web typography (refer to Chapter 9), it's common to indent all paragraphs using the text-indent property (for example, text-indent: 16px). All paragraphs, that is, except the first one, which should have no indent. Here's a rule that uses :first-child to accomplish this:

```
p:first-child {
    text-indent: 0;
}
```

:last-child

The :last-child pseudo-class targets any child element that is the last of a parent element's children:

```
element:last-child {
    property1: value1;
    property2: value2;
    ...
}
```

Note: `element` is the name of the element type you want to target, and it's optional. If you omit `element`, your rule will target everything on the page that's a last child.

For example, one useful design trick is to add some extra whitespace to the bottom of the last paragraph before a heading. Here's a rule that uses `:last-child` to style some extra margin space below every p element that's the last of any parent's children:

```
p:last-child {
    margin-bottom: 24px;
}
```

:nth-child()

The `:nth-child()` pseudo-class selects one or more elements based on their position in a parent element's collection of siblings. Here's the general syntax to use:

```
element:nth-child(n) {
    property1: value1;
    property2: value2;
    ...
}
```

The various parts of this code are as follows:

» `element`: (Optional) The name of the element type you want to target. If you omit `element`, your rule would target everything on the page that's an nth-child.

» `n`: A number, expression, or keyword that specifies the position or positions of the child elements you want to match. There are five main ways to specify `n`:

   • *A* (an integer): Selects the child element in the *A*th position. For example, `p:nth-child(2)` selects any p element that's the second child of a parent.

   • *An* (an integer multiple): Selects every *A*th child element. For example, `p:nth-child(3n)` selects any p element that's in the third, sixth, ninth, and so on, position of a parent's child elements.

- *An+B* (an integer multiple plus an integer offset): Selects every child element that is in the *A*th position, plus *B*. For example, `p:nth-child(3n+2)` selects any p element that's in the second (n=0), fifth (n=1), eighth (n=2), and so on, position of a parent's child elements.

- even (keyword): Selects all the sibling elements that are in even-numbered positions (2, 4, 6, and so on). For example, `p:nth-child(even)` selects any p element that is in an even-numbered position within a parent's child elements. This is equivalent to `p:nth-child(2n)`.

- odd (keyword): Selects all the sibling elements that are in odd-numbered positions (1, 3, 5, and so on). For example, `p:nth-child(odd)` selects any p element that is in an odd-numbered position within a parent's child elements. This is equivalent to `p:nth-child(2n+1)`.

Here's a selector that targets just the even `tr` elements of a parent `table` element:

```
tr:nth-child(even) {
    background-color: lightgray;
}
```

The rule sets the background color of the matching rows to `lightgray`, which produces the effect shown in Figure 6-2.

← → C 🔒 paulmcfedries.com/htmlcssjs/bk03ch02/example17.html

Table 1.1 lists five countries that have a goat population that's larger than their human population.

Country	Goats	People
Somalia	20,500,000	2,300,000
Mongolia	5,126,000	2,300,000
Mauritania	3,310,000	2,100,000
Namibia	1,500,000	1,400,000
Djibouti	504,000	400,000

FIGURE 6-2: Using `nth-child(even)` to style every second row in a table.

When you're counting the child element positions within a parent, you do so regardless of the element type. Consider the following HTML snippet:

```
<section>
    <p>Some paragraph text</p>
    <aside>Some sidebar text</aside>
    <p>More paragraph text</p>
</section>
```

The parent section element has three child elements: a p in position 1, then an aside in position 2, then another p in position 3. A selector such as p:nth-child(3) would successfully match the p element in position 3, but something like p:nth-child(even) would match nothing because there are no p elements in even positions within the section parent.

The :nth-child() pseudo-class has a second syntax that you might find useful:

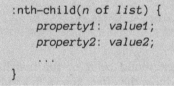

```
:nth-child(n of list) {
    property1: value1;
    property2: value2;
    ...
}
```

The various parts of this code are as follows:

➤ *n*: A number, expression, or keyword that specifies the position or positions of the child elements you want to match.
➤ *list*: A comma-separated list of selectors.

With this syntax, :nth-child(*n* of *list*) matches the expression *n* only for child elements that match one of the selectors in *list*. For example, the following selector matches those even elements that are h1 or h2:

```
:nth-child(even of h1, h2)
```

:nth-last-child()

The :nth-last-child() pseudo-class selects one or more elements based on their position in a parent element's collection of siblings, counting from the end. Here's the general syntax to use:

```
element:nth-last-child(n [of list]) {
    property1: value1;
    property2: value2;
    ...
}
```

The various parts of this code are as follows:

» *element*: (Optional) The name of the element type you want to target. If you omit *element*, your rule would target everything that's an nth-last child.

» *n*: A number, expression, or keyword that specifies the position or positions of the child elements you want to match. You specify *n* using the same methods as I outline in the previous section for the :nth-child() pseudo-class.

» *list*: (Optional) A comma-separated list of selectors.

In short, :nth-last-child() is the same as :nth-child(), except the positions of the parent's child elements are counted starting from the last child, which is in position 1, the second-last child, which is in position 2, and so on.

Chapter **7**

Taking the Measure of CSS

I n this chapter, you replace your artist's beret with your engineer's hard hat and dive into the world of CSS measurement units. Happily, although CSS seems to support an endless number of units, you learn in this chapter that for your everyday CSS needs, there are just a few units that you need to be familiar with.

Getting to Know the CSS Measurement Units

Many CSS properties require a value that's a measure of some kind. For example, a border takes a length value that determines the width of that border. Similarly, a block element can take a dimensional value that sets the block's width or height. Values such as length or dimension are called *measurement values*, and they're essential not only to box model components such as padding, borders, margins, width, and height, but also for many other CSS features, including font sizes, shadow widths, and line spacing.

Almost every measurement value requires a *measurement unit*, which is a short code that specifies which unit you want the browser to apply to a measure. (I lead that previous sentence with "almost" because some properties — such as line-height — take unitless values.) So far in this book, I've talked about measures expressed in pixels, which are designated by the px unit:

```
footer {
    max-height: 200px;
    max-width: 150px;
}
```

However, CSS offers quite a few more measurement units. Most of them are hopelessly obscure or niche, so over the next few sections, I tell you which measurements you need to know.

Learning the Absolute Measurement Units

An *absolute* measurement unit is one that has a fixed size. For example, the px (pixel) unit is defined as 1/96 of an inch. Some web designers prefer absolute measures because they feel it gives them more control over their designs. However, as I explain next, in the "Learning the Relative Measurement Units" section, many web developers are moving away from absolute measurement units because they're too rigid.

Table 7-1 lists all the CSS absolute measurement units.

TABLE 7-1 CSS Absolute Measurement Units

Unit	Name	Equals
px	pixels	1/96 of an inch
pt	points	1/72 of an inch
cm	centimeters	37.8px or about 0.4in
mm	millimeters	1/10 of a cm; about 3.8px
Q	quarter-millimeter	1/40 of a cm; about 1px
in	inches	96px; about 2.54cm
pc	picas	1/6 of an inch; 16px

Of these units, px is by far the most used, with a few designers employing pt and cm on occasion when they're writing CSS for documents that will be printed. If you're going to use absolute measurements and you're writing your CSS only for documents that will display on a screen, stick with px.

My recommendations:

>> It's fine to use px for very small lengths such as those used with most borders and outlines because it makes sense for these widths to be absolute values.

>> Don't use px (or any absolute measurement unit) for anything else.

>> Never, ever use px for font sizes. Why not? Because you make your web page less accessible to people with visual impairments that require them to pump up their web browser's default font size. If they customize the default font size to, say, 32px, and you add a declaration such as font-size: 12px to your html element, you're preventing those folks from experiencing your page text as they wish. Sure, the user can zoom the page, but why would you force them to do that? If you care about accessibility (and I know you do), shun pixel-based font sizes like the plague that they are.

Learning the Relative Measurement Units

A *relative* unit is one that doesn't have a fixed size. Instead, the size depends on — that is, is relative to — something else. The relative unit sizes are measured as outlined in Table 7-2.

Of these, I only recommend spending any time with %, em, rem, as well as the viewport units, all of which I cover in more detail in the sections that follow.

TABLE 7-2 CSS Relative Measurement Units

Unit	Name	Measured Relative To
%	percentage	A quantity defined on the same element or an ancestor element. (The specific quantity depends on the CSS property you're working with.)
em	M-width	The element's inherited or defined font size. The term *em* comes from print typography, where it referred to the width of the capital letter *M*.
ex	x-height	The x-height of the element's font. The *x-height* refers to the height of the lowercase *x* in a specified font.
ch	0-width	The width of the number 0 in the element's font.
rem	root em	The font size of the root element of the web page.
vw	viewport width	1/100 of the viewport width.
vh	viewport height	1/100 of the viewport height.
vmin	viewport minimum	1/100 of the viewport's smaller dimension.
vmax	viewport maximum	1/100 of the viewport's larger dimension.

Playing with percentages

One quick way to get your page elements to behave nicely on screens of different sizes is to express CSS lengths as percentage values. Percentages work well because they're usually calculated relative to the same property in an element's parent. For example, by default a child block element takes up the full width of its parent block. If you want that child element to use only half its parent's width, you set up a rule like this:

```
child {
    width: 50%;
}
```

This is a screen-friendly approach because as the parent block's size changes (say, because the user is resizing the browser window or changing the screen orientation), the child element's width changes along with it to maintain that 50 percent ratio.

One gotcha to watch out for when using percentages is that sometimes what the percentage is relative to is not what you'd expect. For example, when setting padding-top, padding-bottom, margin-top, or margin-bottom, you'd think that these vertical-spacing values would be relative to the parent container's height. Nope. They're actually calculated relative to the parent's *width*, which can lead to some unexpected behavior if you don't allow for this in your declarations.

Trying on the em unit for size

To understand the em measurement unit, you first need to know that CSS uses the font-size property to set the type size for an element. Here's an example:

```
article {
    font-size: 24px;
}
```

REMEMBER

I'm using an absolute value here, which is bad CSS practice, as I explain earlier in this chapter, in the "Learning the Absolute Measurement Units" section.

Second, you also need to bear in mind that font-size is an inherited property so, unless specified otherwise, a child element will always use the same font-size value as its parent.

With those preliminaries out of the way, I can tell you that the em unit takes its value relative to the calculated font size of whatever element you're working with. (This is why em is described as a *font-relative* unit.)

That calculated font size will be either of the following:

>> **A font size inherited by the element:** The inherited font size will be the value of the font-size property defined on the element's closest ancestor that has a font-size declaration. If no ancestor element has a font-size declaration, the inherited font size will be the default font size. (That is, the default size specified by the web browser or the customized default size set by the user.)

>> **A font size defined on the element:** The defined font size is the value of a font-size declaration that targets the element directly.

So, which of these calculated font sizes does the em unit use? Just to thoroughly confuse us all, it depends on what CSS property you're working with! There are, mercifully, just two possibilities:

>> If you're working with an element's font-size property (and a few other typography-related properties, such as text-indent), the em unit is relative to the element's inherited font size. In this case, you can interpret the em unit to mean "the font-size value of this element's parent."

>> If you're working with any other property (such as width, margin, or padding), the em unit is relative to the element's defined font size. In this case, you can interpret the em unit to mean "the font-size value of this element."

In theory, these possibilities make some sense. For example, if you want some child element to use a slightly smaller font size than its parent, you can set up a rule along these lines:

```
child {
    font-size: 0.75em;
}
```

Similarly, it makes sense for properties such as width and padding to scale up or down along with the font size of the element.

In practice, however, em units can be tricky in the extreme, so most CSS designers opt for rem units, discussed next.

Making your life easier with the rem unit

Like em, the rem unit is also font-relative, but the value of rem is relative to just one thing: the font size of the html — also called the *root* — element. What is root font size? It can be any one of the following (in ascending order of weight):

>> The default font size as specified by the web browser. In all modern browsers, that default size is 16px.

>> The custom font size that the user has modified via the web browser's settings. For example, if the user changes

Chrome's Font Size setting to 24px, as shown in Figure 7-1, the root font size becomes 24px.

>> The font-size value that your CSS code sets on the html element.

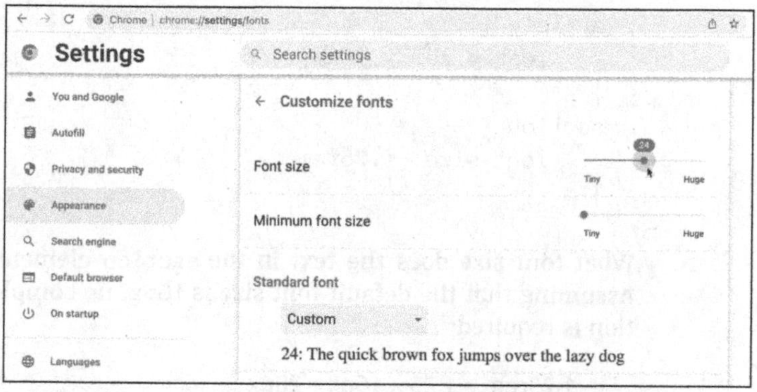

FIGURE 7-1: Users can (and very often do) modify the default font size in the web browser's settings.

Your defined font-size value for the html element takes precedence over any custom value set by the user, so the accessibility-friendly thing to do is to either not include a font-size declaration in the html element or, as is common practice nowadays, set the font-size to 100% to ensure that you're starting with the user's preferred size:

```
html {
    font-size: 100%;
}
```

To understand how easy rem units can make things, here's some code:

HTML:

```
<body>
    <main>
        <article>
            <section>
                What font size am I?
            </section>
```

```
        </article>
    </main>
</body>
```

CSS:

```
article {
    font-size: 1.5rem;
}
section {
    font-size: 1.25rem;
}
```

What font size does the text in the section element use now? Assuming that the default font size is 16px, no complex calculation is required:

1.25rem = 1.25 × 16px = 20px

This calculation will be true no matter which element has the declaration font-size: 1.25rem and no matter what font size is used by the element's parent or ancestors (except, of course, for the ultimate ancestor: the html element).

What if the user has set the default font size to something other than 16px? The use of the rem unit ensures that your text will scale accordingly. For example, if the default font size is now 24px, the calculation becomes the following:

1.25rem = 1.25 × 24px = 30px

And this scaling applies to not just the font-size property but also any property that uses a length measure, such as the margins. For example, if the default font size is 24px, the following code means that the margins around the aside element will also be 24px:

```
aside {
    margin: 1rem;
}
```

So, does this mean that you should always use rem units? Not necessarily. Here are my recommendations:

» Except for the html element (where you should declare font-size: 100%), use rem units for all other font sizes.

» Use rem for all properties that create whitespace on your page, such as margin and padding. Doing so will give your page a consistent look throughout.

» Assume that the user will change the default font size and plan accordingly, which means doing two things:

• If it makes sense for a particular length measurement (such as an element's margins) to scale along with the change in the default font size, declare that measurement with rem units.

• If you don't want a particular length measurement to scale along with the default font size, declare that measurement with any unit that isn't font-relative (such as px, %, or one of the viewport units I discuss in the next section).

» If you want a child element's properties that use font-based values to scale along with changes in the parent's font size, use em units for the child properties. Then, to minimize the effect of compounding due to inheritance, declare the parent element's font size using rem units.

Taking the browser into account with viewport units

From a CSS perspective, the *viewport* is the rectangle (known officially as the *initial containing block*) defined by the html (root) element, which by definition extends the full width and height of the browser window, minus the browser's *chrome* — that is, its user interface features such as the toolbar, address bar, and bookmarks bar. The viewport, in other words, is that part of the browser window through which the visible part of the current web page appears.

CSS includes several so-called *viewport-percentage* units, which are relative to some dimension of the viewport, as shown earlier in Table 7-2.

Here's an example:

```
article {
    width: 75vw;
}
```

Here, the width of the `article` element takes up three-quarters of the width of the viewport.

Viewport-based measures look a lot like percentages (because, say, 1vw is defined as one percent of the viewport width), but viewport units are more straightforward to use because they're relative to just one thing: a viewport dimension. A percentage, by contrast, is usually applied relative to some aspect of the parent element, such as its width. This can lead to unintuitive results such as an element's top and bottom padding changing if the parent element's width changes.

The other advantage of viewport units is that they automatically scale along with the changing viewport size. If the user changes the size of the browser window or rotates their device to a different orientation, a property that uses a viewport-based unit will automatically scale to match the new viewport width or height.

Chapter **8**

Decorating Element Colors and Backgrounds

I n this chapter, you investigate the amazing world of CSS colors. You learn various ways to specify colors, and then you put that newfound know-how to work right away using color to style your text. From there you learn how to set a page background color or image. It's a veritable feast for the eyes, so dive right in.

Picking Out Colors in CSS

When rendering the page using their default styles, browsers don't do much with colors, other than show link text in a default and familiar blue. But CSS offers a ton of properties, keywords, and functions that enable you to add a splash (or even a torrent, if that's your thing) of color to your pages.

The next few sections take you through the main ways that CSS offers to specify a color as a property value.

Working with color keywords

CSS defines more than 140 *color keywords*, which are predefined terms, each of which corresponds to a specific color. Some of the keywords are straightforward and readily grasped, such as `red`, `yellow`, and `purple`. Others are, well, a bit whimsical (and hunger-inducing): `lemonchiffon`, `blanchedalmond`, and `mintcream`. My WebDev Workshop lists them all, as shown in part in Figure 8-1 (surf over to `https://webdevworkshop.io/ck`).

Color	Keyword	RGB	Red	Green	Blue	Hue	Sat	Lum
	lightpink	#ffb6c1	255	182	193	350	100%	86%
	pink	#ffc0cb	255	192	203	349	100%	88%
	crimson	#dc143c	220	20	60	347	83%	47%
	lavenderblush	#fff0f5	255	240	245	339	100%	97%
	palevioletred	#db7093	219	112	147	339	60%	65%
	hotpink	#ff69b4	255	105	180	329	100%	71%
	deeppink	#ff1493	255	20	147	327	100%	54%
	mediumvioletred	#c71585	199	21	133	321	81%	43%
	orchid	#da70d6	218	112	214	301	59%	65%
	thistle	#d8bfd8	216	191	216	299	24%	80%
	plum	#dda0dd	221	160	221	299	47%	75%
	violet	#ee82ee	238	130	238	299	76%	72%
	magenta	#ff00ff	255	0	255	299	100%	50%
	fuchsia	#ff00ff	255	0	255	299	100%	50%

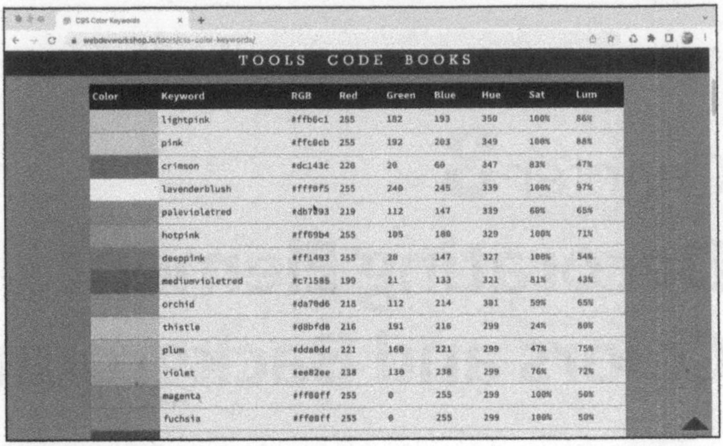

FIGURE 8-1: Go to my WebDev Workshop to check out a full list of the CSS color keywords.

REMEMBER

The CSS color keywords are case insensitive, so the values `red`, `RED`, and even `ReD` all refer to the same color.

Wielding the rgb() function

You may know that you can specify just about any color in the rainbow by mixing three hues: red, green, and blue. Here are some examples:

- Mixing pure red and pure green produces yellow
- Mixing pure green and pure blue produces cyan
- Mixing pure red and pure blue produces magenta
- Mixing all three pure colors produces white

In CSS, you indicate the "pureness" of a color with a number between 0 and 255, where 255 represents the color at its highest intensity (most pure) and 0 represents the color at its lowest intensity (least pure).

To specify any color by mixing red, green, and blue, you can use the rgb() function:

```
rgb(red green blue / alpha)
```

The various parts of this code are as follows:

>> *red*: A number from 0 to 255 (or a percentage from 0% to 100%) that specifies the intensity of the red portion of the final color.

>> *green*: A number from 0 to 255 (or a percentage from 0% to 100%) that specifies the intensity of the green portion of the final color.

>> *blue*: A number from 0 to 255 (or a percentage from 0% to 100%) that specifies the intensity of the blue portion of the final color.

>> *alpha*: A number from 0 to 1 or a percentage from 0% to 100% that specifies the *opacity*, which is a measure of how opaque the color is (where 0 or 0% means completely transparent and 1 or 100% means completely opaque).

TIP

Rather than use 0 or 0% for the *alpha* parameter to make something completely transparent, you can replace the entire rgb() function with the transparent keyword.

Amazingly, these combinations can produce around 16 million colors. For example, the following function produces a nice red (the same red, actually, as the tomato color keyword):

```
rgb(255 99 71)
```

If you want a bit of whatever's behind the element to show through the color, you can add an opacity value, like so:

```
rgb(255 99 71 / 90%)
```

Figuring out RGB codes

An *RGB code* is a hash symbol (#) followed by a six-digit value that takes the form *rdgrbl*, where *rd* is a two-digit value that specifies the red component of the color, *gr* is a two-digit value that specifies the green component, and *bl* is a two-digit value that specifies the blue component.

Sounds reasonable, am I right? Not so fast. These two-digit values are, in fact, *hexadecimal* — that is, base 16 — values, which run from 0 to 9 and then from a to f. As two-digit values, the decimal values 0 through 255 are represented as 00 through ff in hexadecimal.

For example, the following RGB code produces the same red as the function rgb(255 99 71):

```
#ff6347
```

Giving the hsl() function a whirl

If you read the previous two sections, you may now be thinking, "Wow, there's *nothing* intuitive about any of this!" I couldn't agree more. RGB codes are pure High Geekery, and even the mixing of red, green, and blue using the rgb() function is tough to fathom unless you've got a great sense of how color mixing works.

The unintuitive nature of the RGB method of specifying colors has led many CSS developers — amateurs and pros alike — to embrace a different color model that's based on three attributes:

>> **hue:** The color or, more specifically, the position on the color wheel (shown in Figure 8-2), where red is defined as 0 degrees and the colors progress around the wheel to yellow (60 degrees), green (120 degrees), cyan (180 degrees), blue (240 degrees), and magenta (300 degrees), and, of course, everything in between.

>> **saturation:** The purity of the hue, where full saturation means the hue is a pure color and no saturation means the hue is part of the grayscale.

>> **lightness:** How light or dark the hue is, where full lightness produces white and no lightness produces black.

This is the HSL color model and it's much more intuitive because you specify a color with a single value (hue) based on a familiar (or at least comprehensible) mechanism: the color wheel. You then adjust the saturation and lightness to get the color you want.

To work with the HSL color model in CSS, you use the hsl() function:

```
hsl(hue saturation lightness / alpha)
```

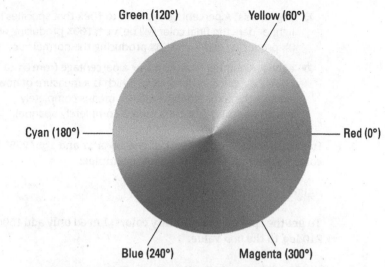

FIGURE 8-2: In the HSL color model, hue refers to a color's position on the color wheel.

The various parts of this code are as follows:

- » *hue*: The position on the color wheel of the hue you want to use as the basis of the color, using one of the following angle units:

  - deg: An angle in degrees, usually from 0 to 359, but negative values and values of 360 or more are legal. For example, the negative value –60deg is the same as 300deg, and the value 480deg is the same as 120deg. This is the default unit, so if you leave it off, the browser interprets your value as an angle in degrees.

  - rad: An angle in radians, usually from 0 to 6.2832 (that is, 2π), but any positive or negative value is allowed.

  - grad: An angle in gradians. A complete circle is 400grad.

  - turn: An angle in number of turns around the color wheel. A complete circle is 1turn; halfway around (180 degrees) is 0.5turn, and so on.

- » *saturation*: A percentage from 0% to 100% that specifies how much of the *hue* is present in the final color, with 100% meaning completely saturated and 0% meaning completely unsaturated (in which case you get a color on the grayscale).

>> *lightness*: A percentage from 0% to 100% that specifies how light or dark the final color will be, with 100% producing white, 0% producing black, and 50% producing the normal *hue*.

>> *alpha*: A number from 0 to 1 or a percentage from 0% to 100% that specifies the *opacity*, which is a measure of how opaque the color is (where 0 or 0% means completely transparent and 1 or 100% means completely opaque).

Here's the hsl() equivalent of the tomato and rgb(255 99 71) color values that I used as earlier examples:

```
hsl(9deg 100% 64%)
```

To get the split complementary colors, I need only add 150deg and 210deg to the *hue* value:

```
hsl(159deg 100% 64%)
hsl(219deg 100% 64%)
```

Coloring Page Text

To apply a CSS color to some text, you use the color property:

```
color: value;
```

Note: *value* is a color keyword, rgb() function, RGB code, or hsl() function.

The following example sets the text color of the aside element to the dark blue given by hsl(209deg 50% 30%):

```
aside {
    color: hsl(209deg 50% 30%);
}
```

Styling Background Colors and Images

By default, every element is given a transparent background. However, CSS comes with a slew of background-related properties that enable you to perk up that default nothingness with either a color or even an image. The next couple of sections take you through the details.

Coloring an element's background

For some extra page pizazz, try adding a color to the background of an element. You do this in CSS by using the background-color property:

```
background-color: value;
```

Note: value is a color keyword, rgb() function, RGB code, or hsl() function.

The following example displays the aside element with white text on a black background:

```
aside {
    background-color: hsl(0, 0%, 0%);
    color: hsl(0 0% 100%);
}
```

When you're messing around with text and background colors, make sure you leave enough contrast between the text and background to ensure that your page visitors can still read the text without shaking their fists at you.

WARNING

Adding a background image

To give your element backgrounds a bit more oomph, you can cover them with an image by setting the element's background-image property:

```
background-image: image;
```

Note: image is the image you want to display as the element background. You have multiple ways to specify the image, but the following two are the most common:

>> **Image file:** Use url("*file*"), where *file* is the filename of the image, including the directory path if the file doesn't reside in the same directory as the file where your CSS code lives.

>> **Gradient:** Specify the gradient using a gradient function such as linear-gradient() or radial-gradient().

Here's an example that adds a background image to a div element:

HTML:

```
<body>
    <div>
    </div>
</body>
```

CSS:

```
div {
    background-image: url("images/webdev-workshop.
    png");
    border: 1px solid black;
    height: 75vh;
    width: 75vw;
}
```

Figure 8-3 shows the result. Notice that when the image is smaller than the dimensions of the target element, the browser repeats — or *tiles* — the image to fill the background.

FIGURE 8-3: The browser tiles smaller images to fill the element's background.

When you use an image as the background of an element that contains text, make sure the image isn't so busy that it makes the element text hard to decipher.

Here's another example of using an image as the background of the body element:

```
body {
    margin: 0;
    font-size: 100%;
    background-image: url("images/ant-on-a-flower.
jpg");
    height: 100vh;
    width: 100vw;
}
```

As shown in Figure 8-4, when you use an image that's larger than the element's dimensions, the browser uses the image to fill the entire background and then lops off the rest of the image.

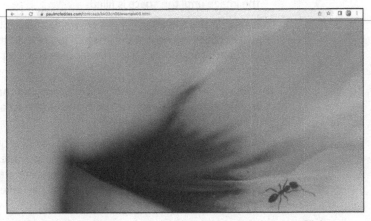

FIGURE 8-4: The browser uses only enough of a larger image to fill the element background.

To control background image characteristics such as how (and whether) a smaller image tiles and how a larger image fits its element's background, CSS offers an alarming number of properties related to background images. Here's a look at the most useful ones:

» background-position: *x y*: Specifies the starting position of the background image, where *x* is the horizontal starting position and *y* is the vertical starting position. Both *x* and *y* can be a keyword (top, right, bottom, left, or center), a percentage, or a length value (such as 50px or 5rem). The default value is left top.

» background-size: *width height* | *keyword*: Specifies the size of the background image. Both *width* and *height* can be a percentage or a length value (such as 250px or 15rem). You can also specify just the *width* value and the browser adjusts the height automatically to keep the image's initial aspect ratio. Alternatively, you can specify a *keyword*, which can be either of the following:

 • contain: Scales the image until it reaches the full width or height of the element (whichever happens first). If space is still left in the other dimension, the browser tiles the image until the space is filled.

 • cover: Scales the image until it covers the full width and height of the element. If the image is larger than the element's background, the browser crops the rest of the image.

The default value is auto auto (which means that the browser automatically sets the width and height according to the image's intrinsic dimensions).

» background-repeat: *horizontal vertical*: Specifies whether and how the background image repeats (tiles) when the image is smaller than the element background (refer to Figure 8-5). Both *horizontal* and *vertical* can take any of the following keywords:

 • repeat: The image repeats along the specified axis (that is, horizontally or vertically) until it fills the available area. If needed, the last repetition of the image will be clipped if there's not enough room to fit the entire image.

 • space: The image repeats along the specified axis without clipping. If there's extra space, the first and last repetitions of the image are pinned to the end of the axis (for example, the left and right ends for the *horizontal* parameter) and the extra space is distributed evenly between the rest of the image repetitions.

- round: The image repeats along the specified axis without clipping. If there's extra space, the image repetitions are stretched in the axis direction to fill that space.

- no-repeat: The image does not repeat along the specified axis.

You can use any of these keywords just once and the browser applies the keyword to both dimensions (for example, background-repeat: space is the same as background-repeat: space space). You can also use the following single-value keywords:

- repeat-x: The image repeats only along the horizontal axis. This is the same as using repeat no-repeat.

- repeat-y: The image repeats only along the vertical axis. This is the same as using no-repeat repeat.

The default value is repeat.

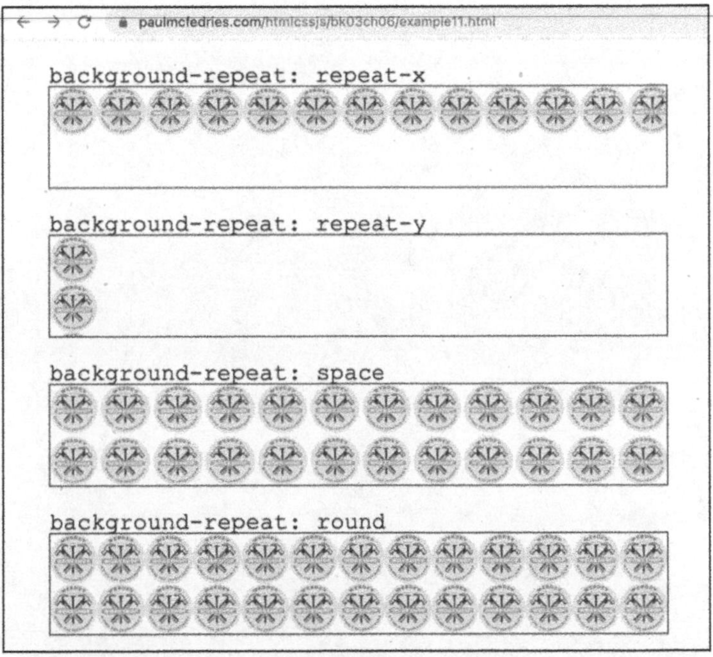

FIGURE 8-5: The various values for background-repeat.

>> background-attachment: *keyword*: Specifies whether the background image scrolls along with the content or remains in place. For *keyword*, use one of the following values:

- local: The image scrolls along with the content.
- scroll: The image is fixed relative to the element.
- fixed: The image is fixed relative to the viewport.

The default value is scroll.

Chapter **9**

Tweaking Text Typographically

I n this chapter, you explore the awesome world of web typography. You learn just enough about typefaces and fonts to be dangerous; how to use beautiful fonts on your web pages; how learning just a few CSS properties can make you a web typography master; and how to fussily align your text just so.

Formatting with Fonts

All web browsers display page text and headings using default styles that are, at best, serviceable. I'm assuming that you're not reading this book because you're the type of person who'll settle for "serviceable." To that end, you can make a huge difference in the overall look and appeal of your web pages by paying attention to the look and appeal of the text itself. This is the beginning of all things typographical, and it's the one thing you need to get right with your page design.

Understanding typefaces

A *typeface* is a particular design applied to all letters, numbers, symbols, and other characters. The most fundamental difference between two typefaces is whether there are small cross-strokes at the extremities of certain characters. These cross-strokes are called *serifs* in the typography game, and Figure 9-1 demonstrates the difference between a character that has serifs and one that doesn't.

Serifs   No serifs

FIGURE 9-1: The letter on the left has serifs; the letter on the right does not.

Typefaces that are decorated with serifs are called — no surprises here — *serif* typefaces, whereas those that lack serifs are called *sans-serif* typefaces (*sans* being a French word that means "without"). So, what does this mean for you when it comes to deciding between one style of typeface and the other? I could probably devote this entire chapter to answering that question, but it really comes down to this:

- » Serifs have a traditional, elegant look, so they're great for more formal web pages or pages trying to project an air of gravity or earnestness.

- » Sans-serifs have a modern, minimalist feel, so they're great for more informal pages or pages looking to project a sense of fun or simplicity.

- » If you've ever been told to use serifs for body text and sans-serifs for headings, forget it. These days, you can switch that advice around or use one kind of typeface for everything on your page.

- » The bottom line is that you should pick a typeface you like, that's readable (many are not!), and that matches the personality of your website.

Okay, you may be asking, if that's a typeface, then what's font? Great question! Many people, even many experienced designers, use the terms interchangeably, but there *is* a difference. A typeface is the overall design used on a set of characters, whereas a *font* is a specific instance or implementation of that typeface. Helvetica is a typeface; 16-point, bold Helvetica is a font.

Styling text with a font family

Even though the entire design world uses the term *typeface* to refer to the general design of a set of characters, the CSS powers that be decided to use the term *font family*. Therefore, the property you use to set text in a specific typeface is named font-family:

```
font-family: name;
```

Here, *name* is the name of the typeface, which needs to be surrounded by quotation marks if the name contains spaces, numbers, or punctuation marks other than a hyphen (-):

```
font-family: "Arial Black";
```

Introducing the font stack

Feel free to list multiple typefaces — thus creating what's known in the trade as a *font stack* — as long as you separate each name with a comma. What's the point of listing multiple typefaces? It gives you more options as a designer. When you list two or more font families, the browser reads the list from left to right, and uses the first font family that's available either on the user's system or in the browser itself.

This left-to-right testing of typeface availability means you can use the following font stack strategy:

```
font-family: ideal, safe, default;
```

The various parts of this code are as follows:

>> *ideal*: This is the name of the font family you'd prefer to use.

>> *safe*: This is the name of a font family that resembles *ideal*, but has a very high chance of being installed on most users' devices.

>> *default*: This is the name of a font family that's similar to *ideal* and *safe*, but is guaranteed to exist, usually because it's part of the web browser itself.

Here's an example font stack:

```
font-family: "Gill Sans", Verdana, sans-serif;
```

When it comes to specifying the families you want to include in your font stack, you have three choices: generic, system, and web.

Formatting text with generic fonts

A *generic* font family is one that's implemented by the browser itself and set by using one of the following five keywords:

>> serif: A serif typeface.

>> sans-serif: A sans-serif typeface.

>> cursive: A typeface designed to look like it was written by hand.

>> fantasy: A decorative font that, depending on the browser, can have some extreme elements (such as wild flourishes).

>> monospace: A so-called *fixed-width* typeface because it gives equal space to each character, so thin letters such as *i* and *l* take up as much space as wider letters such as *m* and *w*.

Figure 9-2 shows each of these generic fonts in action.

As far as your font stack strategy goes, a generic font is perfect for the last font family in the list because you know that it will always be available. So, for example, if your ideal and safe font families are sans-serifs, you include the sans-serif keyword at the end of your font stack.

Formatting text with system fonts

A *system* font family is a typeface that's installed on the user's computer. Almost all system fonts are much nicer than the browser's generic fonts, and you get a wider variety. You also don't take a performance hit because the font is already available for the browser to use.

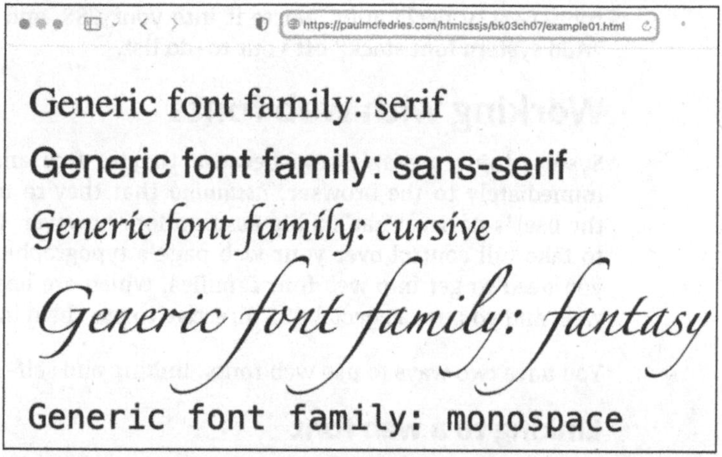

Generic font family: serif

Generic font family: sans-serif

Generic font family: cursive

Generic font family: fantasy

Generic font family: monospace

FIGURE 9-2: Generic fonts are implemented by all web browsers and come in five flavors: serif, sans-serif, cursive, fantasy, and monospace.

How can you possibly know what fonts are installed on each user's system? You can't. Instead, you have two choices. One possibility is to use a system font that's installed universally. Examples include Georgia and Times New Roman (serifs), Verdana and Tahoma (sans serifs), and Courier New (monospace). The other way to go is to use your font stack to list two (or more) system fonts, knowing that the browser will use the first one that's implemented on the user's device. Here's a serif example:

```
font-family: "Big Caslon", Georgia, serif;
```

TIP Some system fonts are installed on at least 90 percent of both Macs and Windows PCs. For sans serif, you can use Arial, Arial Black, Tahoma, Trebuchet MS, or Verdana. For serif, you can use Georgia or Times New Roman. For monospace, it's Courier New. To get the installation percentages for many popular system fonts, surf over to www.cssfontstack.com.

TIP If you want to give your users the familiar feel of their operating system font, use font-family: system-ui, which tells the browser to use the operating system's default font.

TIP A fantastic resource for easily and quickly incorporating system fonts into your page designs is Modern Font Stacks (https://modernfontstacks.com), which offers a collection of system font stacks in various historical typeface classifications (Old Style, Industrial, Antique, and so on). Find a stack you like, copy the `font-family` declaration, paste it into your CSS, and then cross "Add system font stack" off your to-do list.

Working with web fonts

System fonts are awesome because they're free and available immediately to the browser, *assuming* that they're installed on the user's device. That's a big assumption, however. If you want to take full control over your web page's typographical destiny, you need to get into *web* font families, which are hosted on the web, and you use a special CSS directive to use them in your code.

You have two ways to use web fonts: linking and self-hosting.

Linking to a web font

There are quite a few third-party font family providers out there that offer fonts you can link to. Most of these require a license fee. However, if you already have an Adobe account, you have access to Adobe Fonts (`https://fonts.adobe.com`), which offers tons of typefaces.

However, the majority of web designers get their web font families via Google Fonts, which offers access to hundreds of free and well-crafted fonts that you can use on your site. Here's how to choose a font family from Google Fonts:

1. **Surf to** `https://fonts.google.com`.

Figure 9-3 shows the main page of Google Fonts.

FIGURE 9-3: Google Fonts is by far the most popular font provider.

2. Use the Categories list to select the type of font family you want (such as Serif or Monospace).

3. Use the other drop-downs and controls to filter the list as needed.

4. When you come across a font family you like, click it to show the details of the typeface, which includes a list of the available fonts.

5. Click the Select link for each font you want. You'll almost always want just three:

   - Regular 400 (this is regular body text with no italics or bold applied)
   - Regular 400 Italic (regular text with italics)
   - Bold 700 (bold text)

   Refer to "Styling bold," later in this chapter, to learn what numbers such as 400 and 700 mean.

Google Fonts displays a sidebar that lists the choices you've made.

You may be tempted to select every available font, but that's a bad idea because the more fonts you select, the longer it takes to retrieve them all and the slower your web page will load. Unless you have very specific design requirements, you should need only the regular, italic, and bold fonts for a given font family.

6. When you're done with your choices, make sure that the <link> radio button is selected, and then use the Copy icon to copy the code that appears in the box below that radio button (as shown in Figure 9-4).

7. Paste the copied code into your HTML file, somewhere in the <head> section (before your <style> tag, if you're using an internal stylesheet, or before your CSS <link> tag, if you're using an external stylesheet).

8. Return to Google Fonts, scroll down the sidebar until you get to the CSS Rules to Specify Families section, copy that font-family declaration, and then paste that code into each CSS rule where you want to use the font family.

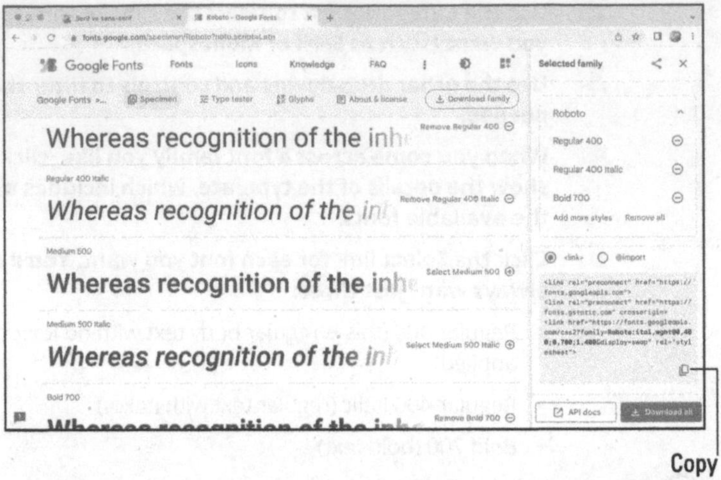

Copy

FIGURE 9-4: When your selections are complete, click Copy to copy the `<link>` code.

Here's an example head section that links to the Google fonts selected in Figure 9-4:

```
<head>
    <meta charset="utf-8">
    <title>Link to a web font family</title>
    <link rel="preconnect" href="https://fonts.
    googleapis.com">
    <link rel="preconnect" href="https://fonts.
    gstatic.com" crossorigin>
    <link href="https://fonts.googleapis.com/css2?
    family=Roboto:ital,wght@0,400;1,400;1,700&display=
    swap" rel="stylesheet">
    <style>
        body {
            font-family: Roboto, Tahoma, sans-serif;
        }
    </style>
</head>
```

In case you're wondering, the first two `<link>` tags enable the browser to fetch the font files right away, so your page loads quicker.

Self-hosting a web font

Using a font provider such as Google is by far the simplest way to stop settling for generic and system font families. With such a wide range of typefaces available, you're sure to find something that makes your pages gleam.

However, you may feel a bit antsy relying on a third-party for such a crucial part of your web design. Most folks have two main concerns here:

>> **The font provider may not provide the font:** Sure, some glitch may cause your provider to fail to deliver the font. However, with a major provider such as Google or Adobe, such failures are extremely rare. And if a glitch does happen, hopefully you've chosen a good system font that will shoulder the typography load.

>> **Delivering a font from the web must be very slow:** This concern seems reasonable because getting anything from a remote server always takes time. However, all font providers have extensive, worldwide delivery networks that serve font files remarkably quickly. And the best of them (such as Google) have come up with ways that, in a sense, preload remote font files, so they're delivered with very little lag time.

The simplicity, reliability, and speed of modern font providers are why most web developers link to remote font files. However, you can also download the necessary font files and host them on your server along with your HTML, CSS, and other files. Hosting your own font files is reliable and fast, but is it simple? Nope, not even close! Here are some things to consider if you're thinking about self-hosting font files:

>> **Typeface licensing:** Almost every commercial typeface either comes with a built-in restriction that prevents the typeface from being used on the web, or requires you to purchase a license that allows web use. Alternatively, you can search the following typeface collections for free or open source typefaces that allow web use:

- Font Space (www.fontspace.com/category/open)
- Font Spring (www.fontspring.com/free)
- Font Squirrel (www.fontsquirrel.com)

- The League of Moveable Type (www.theleagueofmoveable type.com)
- Open Font Library (fontlibrary.org)

>> **File format:** There are tons of font file formats, but these days you have to worry about only one: WOFF2 (Web Open Font Format, version 2), which offers terrific file compression to keep those font files as small as possible.

>> **Getting WOFF2 files:** Unfortunately, when you download a font file from a provider, you won't get WOFF2 files. Instead, you'll likely get either TTF (TrueType Font) or OTF (OpenType Font) files. You could use those, I suppose, but they tend to be five or six times the size of WOFF2 files, so you'd be really slowing down your page load times. Instead, you can use either of the following methods to get WOFF2 files:

- **Google Fonts:** For reasons known only to the Google gods, Google Fonts doesn't offer a simple way to download WOFF2 files. Fortunately, a developer named Mario Ranftl has created a tool called google-webfonts-helper (https://gwfh.mranftl.com/fonts) that enables you to search for a Google font, select the styles you want, and then download a .zip file that contains the WOFF2 files. (It also includes WOFF files, which was the original version of the WOFF type.) In the CSS part of the tool, be sure to click Modern Browsers to get the correct CSS code (more on that code coming up).

- **Font Squirrel:** If you've already downloaded a TTF or OTF file, you can use a Font Squirrel service called the Webfont Generator (www.fontsquirrel.com/tools/webfont-generator), which takes your downloaded font file and automatically creates a package that includes the WOFF2 file format (plus the WOFF file, too). The Webfont Generator package also includes the necessary CSS code to use the fonts on your site.

Okay, so assuming that you now have your WOFF2 files, how do you get them into your CSS? You use the CSS code @font-face (this is a special type of CSS rule called an *at-rule*), and the general syntax takes the following form:

```
@font-face {
    font-family: 'name';
    font-style: style;
    font-weight: weight;
    src: url('filename.woff2') format('woff2')
;
}
```

The various parts of this code are as follows:

- ➤➤ *name*: The name of the typeface.

- ➤➤ *style*: The style of the font, which is usually *normal* or *italic*.

- ➤➤ *weight*: The weight number of the font, such as 400 for regular text and 700 for bold.

- ➤➤ *filename*.woff2: The filename of the WOFF2 font file.

You create a @font-face at-rule for each style and weight you downloaded. Here's an example that sets up three @font-face at-rules for the Roboto typeface:

```
@font-face {
    font-display: swap;
    font-family: 'Roboto';
    font-style: normal;
    font-weight: 400;
    src: url('roboto-regular.woff2')
  format('woff2')
;
}
@font-face {
    font-display: swap;
    font-family: 'Roboto';
    font-style: italic;
    font-weight: 400;
    src: url('roboto-italic.woff2')
  format('woff2')
;
}
@font-face {
    font-display: swap;
    font-family: 'Roboto';
```

```
        font-style: normal;
        font-weight: 700;
        src: url('roboto-700.woff2') format('woff2')
;
}
```

I can then use this in a stylesheet, like so:

```
body {
    font-family: Roboto, Tahoma, sans-serif;
}
```

For best performance, put your @font-face rules in your HTML file's head section, at the beginning of your <style> tag.

The preceding examples assume that you've stored the font files in the same directory as your HTML or CSS file. If you've placed those files in a separate directory, you need to add the correct path information to the url() value:

>> If the font files reside in a subdirectory of the location where the CSS (or HTML) file is stored, precede the filename with the directory name and a backslash (/). For example:

```
url('fonts/roboto-regular.woff2')
```

>> If the font files reside in a subdirectory of the site's root directory, precede the filename with a backslash (/), the directory name, and then another backslash (/). For example:

```
url('/fonts/roboto-regular.woff2')
```

Tweaking the Type Size

Take a look at the page shown in Figure 9-5. To my eye, this page has two main problems, typographically speaking:

>> The typeface is lackluster.

>> The type size is a too small for comfortable reading.

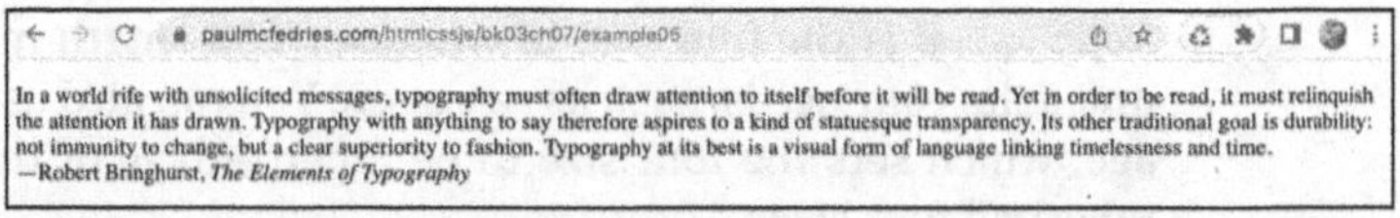

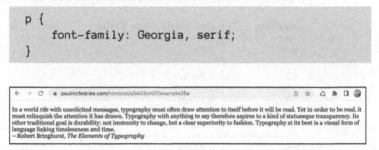

FIGURE 9-5: A typographically terrible web page.

Of these qualities, the typeface is an easy fix because right now the page is just using the browser's default serif typeface. I love the universal system font Georgia, so I modified the page with the following font stack (refer to Figure 9-6):

```css
p {
    font-family: Georgia, serif;
}
```

FIGURE 9-6: The example page with an upgraded typeface.

The biggest problem with typography on the web is that most page text is too small. Why is this problem so widespread? I think there are two main reasons:

» Most web designers just go with the browser's default text size, which is 16px on all modern browsers. The text in Figure 9-5 uses that default 16px size, and it's just too small, especially when seen on a desktop monitor that's a foot or two away from your eyes.

» Print design still has a major influence on web design, which is why I still come across web design gurus recommending that we set our page text at 12px or 14px! Those sizes work fine in print, but they're disastrously small on a web page.

Fortunately, you have total control over the size of your page text via the font-size property:

```css
font-size: value;
```

Note: `value` is the font size in whatever CSS length measurement unit suits your needs, such as `rem` or `em`. You can also use a percentage, which sets the font size to be a percentage of the element's inherited font size.

WARNING

Remember never to use `px` for font sizes because doing so reduces your page's accessibility by overriding the user's custom font size. Always use a relative unit for the `font-size` value.

Besides using `16px` as the default font size for regular page text, modern browsers also use the following default sizes for headings:

Heading	Default font-size Value
h1	2em
h2	1.5em
h3	1.17em
h4	1em
h5	0.83em
h6	0.67em

You can and should override the default browser sizes. For example, I can modify the `p` element that contains the text shown earlier in Figure 9-5 to bump up the `font-size` to `1.25rem`:

```
p {
    font-size: 1.25rem;
}
```

Figure 9-7 shows the result, which is already a marked improvement over the original.

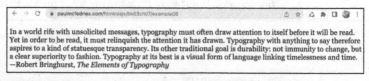

In a world rife with unsolicited messages, typography must often draw attention to itself before it will be read. Yet in order to be read, it must relinquish the attention it has drawn. Typography with anything to say therefore aspires to a kind of statuesque transparency. Its other traditional goal is durability: not immunity to change, but a clear superiority to fashion. Typography at its best is a visual form of language linking timelessness and time. —Robert Bringhurst, *The Elements of Typography*

FIGURE 9-7: The example page with `font-size` set to `1.25rem`.

Styling Text with Bold and Italics

Another typographical touch you can add to your text is to style it with either a different weight or with italics. The next couple of sections take you through the details.

Styling bold text

In CSS, the relative thickness of the strokes that make up a character is called the *weight* of that character. You can control the weight of some page text by applying the font-weight property:

```
font-weight: value;
```

Note: value is a unitless numeric value or keyword that specifies the desired weight:

>> **Numeric value:** Use one of the following: 100, 200, 300, 400, 500, 600, 700, 800, or 900. As shown in Figure 9-8, these numbers apply weights that run from very thin (100) to very thick (900). The labels applied to each weight in Figure 9-8 (Thin, Light, Bold, Black, and so on) are the names you typically come across when examining typeface styles at a font provider. Note that not all typefaces support all the aforementioned values. If a typeface doesn't support a particular weight, the browser will use the closest available weight.

>> **Keyword:** You can use bold instead of 700 and normal instead of 400. To set the weight relative to the parent element's weight, use either lighter (to make the element one weight lighter than the parent; only the weights 100, 400, and 700 are possible with this keyword) or bolder (to make the element one weight heavier than the parent; only the weights 400, 700, and 900 are possible with this keyword).

WARNING

Don't rely on the font-weight property to apply bold to important text or keywords that you want to stand out. In Chapter 3, I talk about how the <strong> and <b> tags have semantic definitions (important text and keywords, respectively), so you should always use those tags to help visitors using assistive technologies. If you want, you can target the strong or b element in your CSS and use font-weight to adjust the weight of those elements.

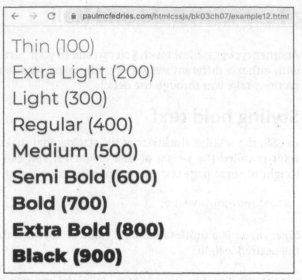

Thin (100)

Extra Light (200)

Light (300)

Regular (400)

Medium (500)

Semi Bold (600)

Bold (700)

Extra Bold (800)

Black (900)

FIGURE 9-8: The font-weight numeric values as rendered by the browser.

WARNING

Users with poor or low vision may have trouble reading text with a weight of 100 or 200. If you use these lower weights, consider bumping up the font size to make the text easier to read.

Styling italic text

In Chapter 3, I mention that the ‹em› and ‹i› tags have semantic significance (emphasis and alternative text, respectively), but you may have text that should get rendered in italics, but not with emphasis or as alternative text. Examples of such text can include subtitles, captions, table column headings, and footnotes. No problem: Get CSS on the job by adding the font-style property to your rule:

```
font-style: italic;
```

As an alternative to the italic value, you can also specify oblique to slant the regular text.

```
font-style: oblique
```

However, because oblique text is just regular text rendered at an angle, oblique text tends to be less attractive than italic text, which is usually a specially designed font.

Aligning Text Just So

When you think about typography (you *do* think about typography, right?), it's natural to think mostly of typefaces and type sizes and type styles. I mean, *type* is right there (sort of) in the word *typography*. That's all great stuff, but I think of these type-related aspects as the *trees* of typography. But there's also a whole *forest* of typography that looks at the bigger picture of the web page. This forest view is, mostly, about aligning things in a satisfying way. Fortunately, CSS comes with a few properties that give you quite a bit of control over how your text lines up.

Setting text alignment

By default, the text inside your page's block-level elements lines up nice and neat along the left edge of the content block. Nothing wrong with that, but what if you want things to align along the right edge, instead? Or perhaps you want to center something within its container. Wouldn't that be nice? You can do all that and more by pulling out the text-align property:

```
text-align: keyword;
```

Note: keyword is the alignment you want to apply. You can use left (the default), right, center, or justify (which aligns the element's text with both the left and right margin).

Figure 9-9 shows the text-align property at work, with paragraphs styled as, from left to right, left, right, center, and justify.

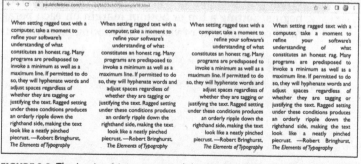

FIGURE 9-9: The text-align property doing its thing (left to right): left-aligning, centering, right-aligning, and justifying.

Hyphenating text

In Figure 9-9, consider the paragraph on the far right that's styled with text-align: justify. This paragraph contains yawning chasms of open space, particularly on the third and fourth lines. Alas, most web browsers aren't very good at justifying text, so these unsightly gaps often occur, especially with shorter line lengths.

You could simply not justify your text, but if you really like the otherwise neat look of justified text, you can give the browser a bit of help justifying the text by letting it hyphenate words as needed. You do that by styling the element with the hyphens property:

```
hyphens: keyword;
```

Note: keyword is the type of hyphenation you want the browser to use. The default is none, but you can tell the browser to go ahead and break words as needed by using the auto keyword. (A third option, manual, enables you to specify your own word-break suggestions by inserting ­, which is the HTML code for a soft hyphen.)

Figure 9-10 shows two paragraphs: the one on the left uses text-align: justify with no hyphenation, whereas the paragraph on the right uses both text-align: justify and hyphens: auto. Letting the browser hyphenate words makes a big difference in both the look and the readability of the text.

Indenting first lines

If your page includes long stretches of text divided into paragraphs, you need to help the reader by offering some kind of visual clue that shows where one paragraph ends and the other begins. Setting a top or bottom margin on each paragraph is the most common way of visually separating paragraphs:

```
p {
    margin 1rem auto;
}
```

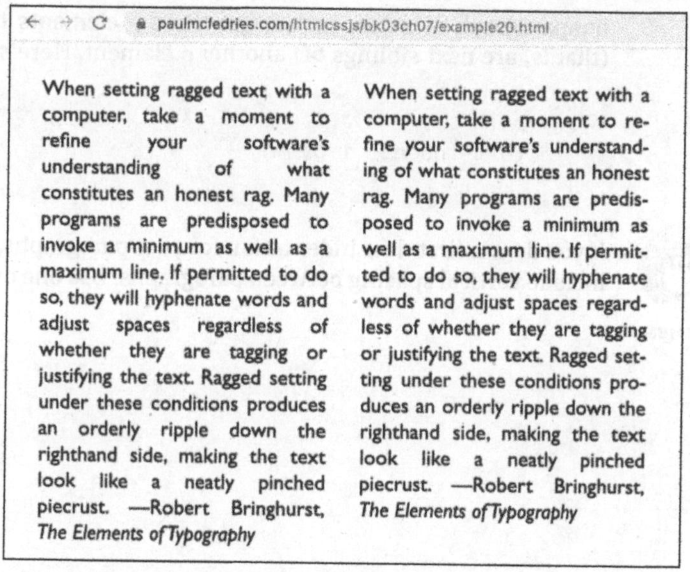

When setting ragged text with a computer, take a moment to refine your software's understanding of what constitutes an honest rag. Many programs are predisposed to invoke a minimum as well as a maximum line. If permitted to do so, they will hyphenate words and adjust spaces regardless of whether they are tagging or justifying the text. Ragged setting under these conditions produces an orderly ripple down the righthand side, making the text look like a neatly pinched piecrust. —Robert Bringhurst, *The Elements of Typography*

When setting ragged text with a computer, take a moment to refine your software's understanding of what constitutes an honest rag. Many programs are predisposed to invoke a minimum as well as a maximum line. If permitted to do so, they will hyphenate words and adjust spaces regardless of whether they are tagging or justifying the text. Ragged setting under these conditions produces an orderly ripple down the righthand side, making the text look like a neatly pinched piecrust. —Robert Bringhurst, *The Elements of Typography*

FIGURE 9-10: A justified, unhyphenated paragraph (left) and a justified, hyphenated paragraph (right).

An alternative method is to indent each paragraph's first line using the text-indent property:

```
text-indent: value;
```

Note: value is the length of the indent using your preferred CSS measurement unit. The default value is 0.

REMEMBER

Set the indent to at least the same size as the paragraph's font or to at most the paragraph's line height. For example, if the paragraph's font size is 1rem and the line height is 1.5, set the indent to between 1rem and 1.5rem.

Note that it's considered good typographical practice to never indent the first line of any paragraph that immediately follows a heading, an aside, or a page element such as an image or video.

Fortunately, there's a simple way to set a first-line indent on all p elements except those that follow a heading or some other nonparagraph element: just target those p elements that follow (that is, are next siblings of) another p element. Here's the rule:

```
p + p {
    text-indent: 1.5rem;
}
```

REMEMBER

If you do use first-line indentation for your paragraphs, don't also include vertical spacing between paragraphs. Use one or the other.

Chapter **10**

Ten Must-Memorize CSS Selectors

C SS saves you oodles of time by making it easy to style page elements. CSS becomes even more powerful when you use selectors to specify which elements you want to work with. In this chapter, you learn the ten selectors you need to tape to your cat's forehead so they're always handy.

The Class Selector

If you've used the class attribute to assign a class name to one or more page elements, you can target those elements by using a *class selector:*

```
.class-name {
    property1: value1;
    property2: value2;
    etc.
}
```

The Id Selector

If you've used the id attribute to assign an ID to a page element, you can target that element by using an *id selector:*

```
#id-name {
    property1: value1;
    property2: value2;
    etc.
}
```

The Type Selector

To target every element that uses a particular element name (such as header or div), use the *type selector:*

```
element {
    property1: value1;
    property2: value2;
    etc.
}
```

The Descendant Combinator

To target every element that's contained within (that is, is a descendant of) a specified ancestor element, use the *descendant combinator* (a space):

```
ancestor descendant {
    property1: value1;
    property2: value2;
    etc.
}
```

The Child Combinator

To target every element that resides one level below (that is, is a child of) a specified parent element, use the *child combinator* (>):

```
parent > child {
    property1: value1;
    property2: value2;
    etc.
}
```

The Subsequent-Sibling Combinator

To target every sibling element that follows a reference element, use the *subsequent-sibling combinator* (~):

```
reference ~ target {
    property1: value1;
    property2: value2;
    etc.
}
```

The Next-Sibling Combinator

To target the sibling element that comes immediately after a reference element, use the *next-sibling combinator* (+):

```
reference + target {
    property1: value1;
    property2: value2;
    etc.
}
```

The First-Child Pseudo-Class

To target any child element that's the first of a parent element's children, use the *first-child pseudo-class:*

```
element:first-child {
    property1: value1;
    property2: value2;
    etc.
}
```

The Last-Child Pseudo-Class

To target any child element that's the last of a parent element's children, use the *last-child pseudo-class:*

```
element:last-child {
    property1: value1;
    property2: value2;
    etc.
}
```

The Nth-Child Pseudo-Class

To target any child element that's the *n*th of a parent element's children, use the *nth-child pseudo-class:*

```
element:nth-child(n) {
    property1: value1;
    property2: value2;
    etc.
}
```

Index

borders
  applying, 79–82
  building, 79–84
  in CSS Box models, 75
  rounding, 82–84
bulleted lists, building, 45–46
<button> tag, 56–57
buttons, adding to web forms, 56–57

C

Canva, 50
cascading style sheets (CSS)
  about, 5–6, 15–16, 111
  absolute measurement units,
    112–113
  applying styles to pages, 18–22
  box model
    about, 73–74
    applying borders, 79–82
    block boxes, 75–76
    building borders, 79–84
    components of, 74–75
    inline boxes, 75–76
    margins, 85–86
    padding, 77–78
    rounding borders, 82–84
    specifying maximum/minimum
      height/width, 89–90
    styling sizes, 86–91
  em unit, 115–116
  hsl( ) function, 124–126
  measurement units, 111–112
  percentages, 114–115
  relative measurement units, 113–120
  rem unit, 116–119
  rgb( ) function, 122–123
  rules and declarations, 16–18

selecting colors in, 121–126
selectors
  child combinator, 155
  class attribute, 153
  descendant combinator, 154
  first-child pseudo class, 156
  id attribute, 154
  last-child pseudo-class, 156
  next-sibling combinator, 155
  nth-child pseudo class, 156
  subsequent-sibling combinator, 155
  type, 154
  viewport units, 119–120
case-sensitivity
  for color keywords, 122
  in filenames, 6
ch unit, 114
character entities, 49
character references, 49
characters, handling with <span>, 38
checkboxes, adding to web forms,
  61–64
child combinator (>), 101, 155
child elements, matching, 104–109
chrome, 119
class, 97
class attribute, 153
class selector (.), 97–99
cm unit, 112
colon (:), 17, 103
color picker, 69–70
color property, 126
colors
  background, 126–132
  of borders, 80–82
  keywords for, 121–122
  for page text, 126

id selector (#), 99–100

images
background, 126–132
files for, 127
formats for, 50–51
inserting, 49–53
turning into links, 52–53

‹img› tag, 51

in unit, 112

indenting first lines, 150–152

initial containing block, 119

inline boxes, 75–76

inline element, 38

inline quotation, 42

inline styles, inserting, 18

‹input› tag, 57–60, 61–64, 69–72

inserting
images, 49–53
inline styles, 18
special characters, 48–49

inset keyword, 80

internal style sheets, embedding, 18–21

italic, styling text with, 148

J

Joint Photographic Experts Group (JPEG), 50

K

keywords
about, 87
color, 121–122
defined, 41
for styling bold text, 147

L

‹label› tag, 60–61, 63

labels, adding to web forms, 60–61

:last-child pseudo-class, 105–106, 156

launching text files, 6

The League of Moveable Type, 142

‹legend› tag, 63

less-than symbol (<), 27, 49

‹li›...‹/li› tag, 45–46

licensing typefaces, 141–142

lightness, 124, 126

line breaks, in web pages, 29–30

‹link› tag, 21–22

links
creating, 43–44
turning images into, 52–53
to web fonts, 138–140

local web page, 43

lossy compression, 50

M

macOS
TextEdit, 6
Web browser in, 7

main element, 94

‹main› tag, 33–34

margins
about, 85–86
in CSS Box models, 75

marking text, 41

matching child elements, 104–109

measurement units
about, 111
absolute, 112–113
CSS, 111–112
relative, 113–120

About the Author

Information appears to stew out of me naturally, like the precious ottar of roses out of the otter.

—*Mark Twain*

Paul McFedries is a technical writer who spends his days writing books just like the one you're holding in your hands. In fact, Paul has written more than 100 such books that have sold over four million copies worldwide. Paul invites everyone to drop by his personal website at `https://paulmcfedries.com`, or to follow him on X (`www.twitter.com/paulmcf`) or Facebook (`www.facebook.com/PaulMcFedries`).

Dedication

To Karen, my lobster

Author's Acknowledgments

Each time I complete a book, the publisher sends me a heavy box filled with a few so-called "author" copies. Opening that box, lifting out a book, feeling the satisfying weight of something that has, up to now, been weightlessly digital, and seeing my name printed on the cover, well, it's a pretty fine feeling, let me tell you. That's pretty cool, but you know what's *really* cool? That I've done that over a hundred times in my writing career, and seeing my name on the cover has *never* gotten old.

But just because mine is the only name you see on the cover, doesn't mean this book was a one-man show. Far from it. Sure, I did write this book's text and take its screenshots, but those represent only a part of what constitutes a "book." The rest of it is brought to you by the dedication and professionalism of Wiley's editing, graphics, and production teams, who toiled long and hard to turn my text and images into an actual book.

I offer my heartfelt thanks to everyone at Wiley who made this book possible, but I'd like to extend some special thank-yous to the folks I worked with directly: executive editor Lindsay Berg and editor Elizabeth Kuball.

Publisher's Acknowledgments

Executive Editor: Lindsay Berg

Editor: Elizabeth Kuball

Production Editor:
Saikarthick Kumarasamy

Cover Design and Image: Wiley